A
GUIDE
TO
CONSUMER LAW
THE EASYWAY
David Marsh

Easyway Guides

D1135969

9030 00003 6880 2

Easyway Guides

© Straightforward Publishing 2014

All rights reserved. No part of this publication may be reproduced in a
retrieval system or transmitted by any means, electronic or mechanical,
photocopying or otherwise, without the prior permission of the
copyright holders.

978-1-84716-415-5

Printed by Grosvenor Group London

Cover design by Bookworks Islington

Whilst every effort has been made to ensure that the information
contained within this book is correct at the time of going to press, the
author and publisher can take no responsibility for the errors or
omissions contained within.

LONDON BOROUGH OF WANDSWORTH	
9030 00003 6880 2	
Askews & Holts	13-Feb-2014
343.41071	£8.99
	WWX0011883/0009

CONTENTS

Introduction   8

1. Consumer Protection Generally   12

   The Law of Contract   12
   The Contract of Sale   13

2. Defective Goods/Non Receipt of Goods   16

   Defective goods generally   16
   Delivery of damaged items/Non-receipt of goods   19
   The goods still haven't arrived   19
   The goods have arrived damaged   19
   Sending the goods back   20
   Getting your money back   21
   Charge back on credit and debit cards   21

3. Other Consumer Transactions   24

   General   24
   Use of Materials When Carrying Out Repairs   25
   Example   26
   The Consumer Protection Act 1987   27

4. Guarantees and Warranties   31

   Warranties   31
   Legal Protection Guarantees and Warranties   31
   Frequent Problems   33

....

5. Denying Liability For Products   34

General   34
The Effect of European Decisions   38

....

6. Unsolicited Goods   39

Civil Law   39
Criminal law   40

....

7. Purchasing Goods at Home   41

Buying on the doorstep   41
Criminal Offences   41
Cancelling an agreement   42
Faulty Goods or Services   43
Distance Selling   44
The Right to Clear Information   45
Your Right to Cancel   46
If the Seller Outside UK   47
If the Goods Don't Arrive   47

....

8. Consumers and Credit   49

General   49
What the law says   50
Right of withdrawal   50
Credit Cards   50
Credit reference agencies   51
Credit Unions   51

Hire purchase   52
Logbook loans   52
Money lenders   53
Payday loans   53
Personal loans   54
the Consumer Credit (Advertisement) regulations 2010   55
The Consumer Credit Association (CCA)   60
Consumer Credit Trade Association (CCTA)   61
The Finance and Leasing Association (FLA)   61

9. Defective goods purchased on credit   63

Inability to Meet Repayments   63
The Consumer Credit Act and Extortionate
Credit Bargains   64
The Position When Purchasing Hire Goods   65

10. The Consumer Protection from Unfair Trading
    Regulations 2008   66

The legislation   67
What is prohibited?   67
Misleading actions and omissions   70
Aggressive practices   72
General duty not to trade unfairly   74
Consequences of non-compliance   74

11. Unsafe Goods   76

General   76

12. Package Holidays 79

The Package Travel. Package Holidays and
Package Tours Regulations 1992 79
The Definition of Package Holidays 79
Information Given by Tour Operator 80
Statements Made in Holiday Brochure 81
Liability-Terms and Performance of the Contract 81
Alterations to a Holiday 82
Overbooking of Flights 82
Insolvency of the Tour Operator 83
Consumer Remedies 83
Recent Developments in the Law 84

13. Food Safety 85

General 85
The Food Standards Act 1999 86

14. Consumer Remedies 88

Alternative Dispute Resolution 88
Types of ADR 89
Conciliation 89
Arbitration 89
Mediation 90
Ombudsman Schemes 90
Locating an ADR Scheme 91

The Small Claims Court   91
Commencing a Claim   91
Types of Claim   92

15. Consumer Issues Generally   100

Buying Goods and Services Within Europe   100
Timeshare property   102
Personal Protection insurance (PPI)   105
Travel Insurance   107
Suppliers Going Out of Business   109
Dry Cleaning   110
Mobile Phones   111
Private and Car Boot Sales   113
Buying at Auction   113
Banks and Building Societies   114
Car Insurance   116
Motor cycle insurance   118
Dealing with Builders   119
Saving for Christmas   122

16. Consumer Law in Scotland   125

General   125

Sample letters of complaint
Useful Addresses
Index

INTRODUCTION

The aim of the book is to outline the rights of the consumer when entering into a transaction with a seller of goods, whatever those goods might be. People do not know their rights when encountering problems at the point of sale or after. What, for example, are your rights if goods turn out to be unsuitable or substandard and the seller refuses to let you have your money back or generally try's to tell you that there is nothing that can be done.

There are three legal systems in the United Kingdom: English Law, which covers Wales as well, Scottish law and Northern Irish law. In practice there is very little difference between English law and Northern Irish law so reference throughout this book will be to English law. Scottish law differs significantly. Courts have different procedures and some laws are different. There will be a brief resume of Scottish law in chapter 17.

A main area which causes problems, and is always in the news, is that of consumer credit. The Government has put forward various White Papers which seek to impose a greater regulatory framework on all areas of consumer credit as it is feared that individual borrowing is reaching unacceptable levels. Payday loans are the latest area of lending to undergo scrutiny.

Hire agreements are also covered along with the sale of unsafe goods. Food safety and general hygiene are also outlined. In addition, there is a section that covers general consumer issues such as dealing with banks, mobile phones, dry cleaning, travel insurance and private sales. Finally, there is a new section on saving for Christmas, outlining pro's and cons's of the safest ways to save. This has been introduced specifically following the Farepak debacle where many people lost a lot of money.

The government relatively recently introduced a set of regulations, which are outlined in chapter 11, The Consumer Protection Against Unfair Trading Practices Regulations 2008 governing rogue traders, in particular pressure selling and underhand tactics designed to get people to buy goods. These rules came into force May 2008. They also cover Trade Descriptions and misleading prices. For more information on these rules you should access the Citizens Advice Website, both of these are featured in useful addresses at the back of the book.

The Draft Consumer Rights Bill

At present consumer laws are contained within 8 complicated pieces of legislation, some of which dates back to the 70s. As a result the current laws are difficult for consumers to understand and on many occasions do not fit with the modern internet era, whereby more and more consumers purchase online.

With this being the case, an overhaul of UK consumer laws has been long overdue. In June 2013, the Consumer Minister unveiled a set of proposals, within the 'draft Consumer Rights Bill', which streamlines the current eight pieces of legislation into one consumer Bill. These proposals are designed to make consumer laws easier to understand and ultimately to bring consumer laws into line with the new realities..

Return of Faulty goods for a repair/replacement-Current law

If the retailer cannot prove that the goods were 'fit for purpose' when they were sold you are entitled to a repair or replacement within the first six months. The current law does not provide any confirmation on how many repairs or replacements you have to accept before asking for a refund.

Proposed law

You will still be entitled to a repair or replacement within the first six months if the retailer can't prove the item was fit for purpose when it was sold. However, under the proposed law you will have the right to insist on a refund after one failed repair or one faulty replacement.

Return of Faulty goods for a refund-Current law

If you buy goods that turn out to be faulty you currently have the right to return the goods and demand a full refund within a "reasonable time". Problems that have commonly arisen with this is how long is reasonable? Many retailers state that this is 14 days.

Proposed law

You will have a set 30-day period to return faulty goods and get a full refund.

Cancelling goods/services purchased online or on your doorstep-Current law

The law currently calls this 'distance selling' and under the rules you have what is known as a 7 day 'cooling off period'. This means that you can simply change your mind within 7 days of receiving the goods or ordering a service and demand a full refund.

Proposed law

The law here will remain the same but the 7 day period will increase to 14 working days.

Poor services-Current law

Currently the law does not give consumers the right to demand that a service be put right due to being substandard nor does it provide the right to a refund in these circumstances.

Proposed law

When you receive poor or substandard service you will be able to demand that the service be rectified or get a full or partial refund.

Faulty digital goods (i.e. music and video downloads)-Current law
Currently the law is totally inadequate in this area as it is silent on whether consumers are entitled to a refund when something goes wrong with digital goods.

Proposed law
You will be entitled to demand either a replacement or a full/partial refund.

These are all positive changes that undoubtedly give consumers greater and clearer rights. However, these proposed changes will not become law until at least mid 2014 and of course they rely upon the retailers abiding by them. It is universally recognised that they are also only the start of what is needed to properly drag consumer laws in the 21st Century.

The rights of the consumer are quite considerable and yet most of us live in complete ignorance of exactly what they are. The obligations on those who sell us goods generally are considerable, corresponding with consumer rights.

The primary purpose of this book is to educate the consumer and to empower that person by fostering an understanding of the responsibilities of the seller.

It is hoped that all will benefit by reading this book. The rights of the consumer are of paramount importance and it is one area where general education leaves a lot to be desired.

Chapter 1

Consumer Protection Generally

Consumers are protected by both civil and criminal law. As we shall see below, the general law of contract gives some protection, especially from misrepresentation. There are special rules for consumer contracts, including:

- Contracts for buying goods
- Contracts for services
- Distance selling
- Other areas such as package holidays, insurance, food and finance

The tort of negligence gives limited protection where the consumer has no contractual rights. In addition, there is protection from defective goods under the Consumer Protection Act 1987. The criminal law also affords some protection against such matters as trade descriptions.

The law of contract

All transactions between consumers and suppliers are based on the law of contract. Every exchange of goods is an agreement between buyer and seller.

It therefore follows that underlying each exchange is an area of law which defines the rights and obligations of both buyer and seller. The purchaser and the person who sells goods and services are not free to do exactly as they wish after the sale or, indeed, make up the rules as they go along.

The major area of law which supports and assists consumers is the Sale of Goods Act 1979, as amended by the Sale and Supply of Goods Act 1994. This Act governs all transactions where goods are transferred for a price.

There are, however, certain situations where a consumer will not be covered by the Sale of Goods Act. As was mentioned, this Act covers transactions where a sum of money is involved, where a price has been set for the goods. In some circumstances you may swap or exchange goods. In this case, the transaction will be governed by the Supply of Goods and Services Act 1982.

There are a number of transactions which may involve a combination of swap and cash, such as the trading-in of a product against a newer model. If an amount of cash is involved, no matter how small, then the Sale of Goods Act 1979 will apply.

The contract of sale

There are what is known as "express and implied" conditions governing any contract, not just consumer contracts. Express terms of the contract are those agreed by the buyer and seller. However, once it has been determined that the Sale of Goods Act covers the transaction there are certain conditions implied into the sale by the Act. These conditions cannot be circumvented by the seller.

In every contract for the Sale of Goods, the 1979 Act states that where there is a sale of goods by description there is simultaneously an implied condition that the goods sold will match their description. In other words, the seller must sell you what has been described in the advertising. Nothing more and nothing less will suffice.

Section 13 of the Sale of Goods Act applies to all sales, whether by private individuals or business. Anyone who sells a good to another is covered. Section 13 applies to all goods no matter what the purchasing situation. Just because, for example, the goods were on open display and the potential buyer can see what is on offer, does not mean that sale by

13

description does not apply A tin of fruit might contain a different fruit to what is described in the tin or a sweater might in fact not be 100 per cent wool as it says on the label.

The golden rule which underpins the Act is that the description of the product on offer must match the product sold. As television shopping assumes greater prominence, in the form of television shopper channels, this Act will assume greater importance. No longer will there be the direct face-to-face contact between the buyer and the seller, only a telephone line. The process of challenging the product when you eventually receive it will be more long winded, as it often is with mail order of whatever description. However, consumers will need to be aware of their rights in the probable instance of receiving goods that do not correspond to what was requested. We will be discussing distance selling and the Distance Selling Regulations 2000 further on in this book.

x   There may be cases where the consumer purchases goods and relies on a sample to make a choice. This is quite often the case when choosing fabric for furnishings or carpets. The Sale of Goods Act also covers samples and states that the goods must correspond with the description of those goods and not just the sample shown.

This is very important for those who feel let down by goods received by way of choosing from samples and wish to return those goods. Remember THE SALE OF GOODS ACT 1979 SECTION 13 is the Act that you should refer to if you experience problems in this area.

Your rights under this section entitle you to reject the goods and obtain a refund. It is not at the discretion of the seller, but your right.

In addition to the goods not matching up to the description, section 30 of the Act also provides a remedy to the consumer if quantity of goods is not that which was requested or advertised. Quite simply, because a different amount is supplied then there has been a breach of description.

If the consumer receives a mixture of goods, for example, two saucepans ordered but the third different to the one described then the right exists to reject the goods. There is no right for the consumer to keep the goods. They must be returned if rejected.

****

Chapter 2

Defective Goods/Non-receipt of Goods

In the previous chapter we looked at consumer rights generally and pointed out the importance of the Sale of Goods Act 1979, as amended. In this chapter we will look at the area of law protecting consumers when a good or service supplied is defective, either when you get the goods home, or defective or damaged on delivery or not received at all.

You can ask the seller to replace or repair the goods free of charge if they are faulty. If you do this within six months of receiving the goods, and it is reasonable to expect them to have lasted for the period of time that you have had them, it will be assumed that the problem existed when you bought the goods, unless the seller can demonstrate otherwise. However, you can still ask for a replacement or repair for up to six years from the date that you purchased the goods, if it is reasonable to assume that they should have lasted that long. Obviously, common sense applies here and the longer that you have the goods the more difficult it will be to prove that there was a problem at the time of purchase.

Notwithstanding the above, and sometimes the seller will make life difficult, even going so far as to refuse to exchange goods or refund money.

This is a blatant breach of the law and of the rights of the consumer. Again, it is necessary to be able to quote the law and show that you mean business.

There are many examples of defective goods. This can range from the washing machine or fridge to the item of clothing that either has a defect or does not last the first wash.

The Sale of Goods Act 1979 covers these situations. The seller has to be an established business however. It is most important to understand this point. The Act does not cover private sales. However, the purchaser can be business or private. There is no distinction here.

Goods sold in the course of business must be what is known as "of merchantable quality'. Section 14 of the Sale of Goods Act 1979 defines this. Basically, goods are of a merchantable quality if they are as fit for the purpose for which goods of that kind are commonly bought. In other words, the good must be the same high quality as other goods of a similar kind. If they are not then they are defective.

The price of a good is of significant importance when considering the notion of merchantable quality. A product may be soiled in some way and not achieve the required standard. However, the actual cost of the good is of importance.

Sometimes you buy a good, find that it is defective, take it back and are told by the salesman that it can be repaired quite easily. What is your position then? The position is that you do not have to accept a repair to the item but can demand an exchange or refund. However, there will be cases where the repairing of an item is the only way forward from a practical point of view. This is quite reasonable in the circumstances.

Sometimes, and this is quite common, a guarantee will be given with a product. This gives the consumer an automatic right to a replacement if a good is defective. Guarantees and warranties are discussed further on in this book.

The situation is slightly different when the consumer purchases a second hand item.

The same condition applies as to new goods but obviously age and condition of the item have to be taken into account and the buyer should realise that there is a greater risk of a defect. However, the Sale of Goods Act still applies in the case of second hand goods.

There is however, one proviso here. That is that the Sale of Goods Act says that goods must be of merchantable quality unless the defect is pointed out to the buyer by the seller. Examination of the goods, and the acceptance of those goods provides a get out for many sellers.

This situation can be awkward as many buyers are keen to examine anything they buy. If you miss a defect in a good then the seller has the right to say that you should have noticed the defect. In many cases, of course, the defect may not be readily apparent. If you do examine goods before purchase then it is highly advisable to check thoroughly before acceptance.

The Sale of Goods Act section 14 also governs what is known as "fitness of purpose". Fitness of purpose quite simply means that the goods purchased must be reasonably fit for the purpose for which they are made. For example, a purchase of a dishwashing machine would lead us to believe that we are buying something that can wash dishes. If this is not the case then the consumer has every right to return the goods.

There are examples here, though, where the buyer cannot demand recompense from the seller if he has not relied on the skill and judgement of the seller. A typical example may be where the buyer goes into a shop and demands something that he assumes is compatible with something else, for example, a printer which he asks for by name, receives it and subsequently finds that it is not fit for the purpose. The key is to ask as many questions as possible before purchasing in order to give the seller as much information as is needed to ensure that the good that he is selling is the correct good.

Buyers of goods have to understand the nature and consequences of *acceptance of goods.* The Sale of Goods Act sections 34 and 35 deals with acceptance. Section 35 is very important. Basically, if a buyer accepts goods then any damages payable on subsequently discovering a problem will be affected.

Delivery of damaged items/Non-receipt of goods

With the increase in online shopping comes an obvious increase in the number of complaints regarding delivery of goods – whether this is non-delivery or delivery of damaged items. So where do you stand?

The first point to distinguish is whether you ordered the goods under a distance selling contract, or whether you arranged delivery after buying them in a shop, as this will affect your consumer rights.

The goods still haven't arrived

Under the distance selling regulations, the goods must be delivered within the time period they have specified. If no time period is specified, then the statutory time limit is 30 days (unless you have agreed otherwise). If the supplier is unable to do this, they must inform you before the end of the 30 day deadline. They may offer you an alternative date for delivery, but you are under no obligation to accept and can ask for a full refund. For other purchases, Sale of Goods only refers to 'reasonable time'. If you fear you've been the victim of fraud, refer to 'getting your money back' at the end of this section.

The goods have arrived damaged

As you might expect, the supplier is under obligation to ensure the goods are well protected while they are in transit. The supplier must also make sure the delivery company/courier are aware that the goods are fragile or if they are to be kept or carried in a certain way. If they do not, they will be liable for any damage occurred in transit.

It is common for traders to sidestep liability by saying that you signed for them. A delivery note (as the name suggests) indicates merely that the product has been delivered and not that they have been accepted. If there is a problem with the goods, you may still reject them, particularly if you haven't previously had a chance to examine them in person. With some items you will be asked to inspect the goods there and then and sign a form to say that they have arrived in satisfactory condition. The law states that you should have reasonable opportunity to examine the goods for yourself, so you could argue that 'there and then' is not reasonable and opt not to sign the form. You should however look at the supplier's Terms and Conditions to see whether they have imposed any time limit on reporting faults – although in line with the law, this should be reasonable.

It should be pointed out that if you did have the chance to examine the goods while they still in the shop, and you spot something wrong when it arrives that you should have spotted when you examined it, you may not be able to reject it. Although in reality, most shops will show some good will if you simply want to exchange it for another one.

Sending the goods back

Unless you have bought the goods under a distance selling contract, you won't have any legal right to send the goods back if you have simply changed your mind. You should refer to that retailer's return policy and will probably have to pay postage. If the goods have arrived damaged, and you have been offered or have requested a repair or a replacement, you should not have to pay any further sums of money in this respect. This includes labour, materials or postage. The repair / replacement should take place in 'reasonable time' and you should not experience any 'significant inconvenience', while you are without it/them. In all respects, you will have greater rights if you had bought them under a distance contract (online, mail order). This is because you didn't have the opportunity to examine them before they were shipped – to see if they are:

- Of satisfactory quality

- As described

- Fit for intended purpose

- Appropriate to your requirements

20

With this in mind you will have a 7-day cooling off period, during which time you can cancel the contract and get your money back in full (including delivery charges). Unless otherwise specified (for certain types of products), you should be able to send the items back for free, and not incur any additional charges such as a restocking or admin fee. Although many retailers will request products to be returned in a saleable condition in their original packaging, they cannot make it a condition of giving you a refund. For more on returns and refunds under a distance selling contract, see the section on distance selling and buying online.

Getting your money back

Under Sale of Goods, if the goods are poor quality, unfit or not as described, you may be eligible for an immediate refund, although no definitive timescale is mentioned beyond 'reasonable time'. Under a distance selling contract, your 7 day cooling off period entitles you to a refund within 30 days. If you have not received the goods and suspect you may have been the victim of fraud, you can take it up with your credit card company (provided you paid on credit card and certain conditions are met), or invoke the Visa Debit Chargeback procedure.

Chargeback on credit and debit cards

Chargeback may be possible where section 75 of the Consumer Credit Act 1974 doesn't apply, for example for items of £100 or under, or debit card purchases. (see section on credit cards and loans). Chargeback is a process allowing you to ask your card provider to reverse a transaction if there's a problem with something you've bought.

Chargeback is not enshrined in law like section 75, but is part of Scheme Rules, which participating banks subscribe to.

It applies to all debit cards, although exact rules may vary between the Visa, Maestro and American Express networks.

Chargeback also applies to credit cards and is particularly useful where section 75 is not applicable – for goods costing less than £100, for instance.

When can chargeback be used?

Like section 75, chargeback can be used in cases of goods not arriving, arriving damaged, arriving not as described, or where the merchant has ceased trading.

You can ask your card provider to try to claw back the money you paid or part of it.

If, for example, you ordered two items but only one arrived, you can ask for the money back on the item you didn't receive. But you can't claim back the cost of fixing a faulty item.

Chargeback doesn't mean there is joint liability on the card company in the way that Section 75 does.

Claims must be addressed to the bank that provides your debit or credit card, which in turn will put in a request to the merchant's bank.

As a result, you could get your money back from the merchant's bank if the money is there to be recovered.

But, there are no guarantees your bank will be able to recover the money through chargeback, or that the trader will accept that you were justified in taking the money back. The trader could argue that you're in breach of contract for not paying.

Conditions and requirements of chargeback

The main requirement for getting your money back is evidence that there's been a breach of contract.

There is also a time limit on claims - typically 120 days - which starts from the day you become aware of a problem.

In the case of tangible goods that you've purchased from a high street shop or an online retailer, the time limit would start from the day you receive your items.

In the case of an airline going bust after you've booked a flight, the breach of contract would be from the day the flight was due to depart.

However, if an airline had told you at an earlier date that the flight would not be going ahead, the breach of contract that aPayPal and chargeback

Watch out if you use your credit or debit card to load money into your PayPal account or other similar online accounts, as it is the loading of the money that is considered to be the card transaction.

If the money that you load into your account is then subsequently used to buy goods and services, that transaction is not classed as a card transaction and is unlikely to be covered by chargeback.

If you're making a card purchase through PayPal it's best to empty your PayPal account regularly so there is no credit balance.

That way, when you make a card purchase through PayPal, the same amount will be debited from your bank account or credit card as goes immediately to the seller.

This will make it easier for your bank or credit card provider to match the purchase with the debit.

If you have any trouble when putting in a claim to your credit or debit card provider, try asking to speak to a supervisor.

Chargeback is less well-known than section 75, and some bank staff may not be aware of this rule.

If your card provider rejects your chargeback claim, you can take your case to the Financial Ombudsman Service within six months of your final correspondence.

Chapter 3
Other Consumer Transactions

In chapter two we looked at the law and defective goods, transactions between seller and buyer which are covered by the Sale of Goods Act. However, there are transactions which are not covered by the Act, simply because there is no "transfer of property for a monetary consideration called a price".

An example may be the purchase of a good under a hire purchase agreement. We will be discussing this in more depth later. However, purchase of goods in this way constitutes "bailment". In other words, the goods are owned by the hire purchase company until the last payment is made. If the good is defective in this case, what is the remedy? Hire purchase transactions of this kind are covered by the Supply of Goods (implied terms) Act 1973. Sections 9 and 10 are exactly the same as sections 13 and 14 of the Sale of Goods Act and therefore the remedy lies here.

There is another form of consumer transaction which needs to be understood. This is known as the *conditional sale transaction.* This is where a buyer of a good, a typical example being a car, may have the car for six months and have constant trouble. If the buyer experiences ongoing trouble and the garage is alerted then he will be entitled to a refund of his money.

There is an important point to be made here. That is the buyers attitude and whether or not he accepts the good even though it is defective. Two notions exist - acceptance and affirmation. What this means is that acceptance will occur when the buyer accepts delivery. However, affirmation can only occur when the defect is known, with time starting to run from that point. If the buyer simply carries on driving the car, or using the good even though there is knowledge of the defect then he is accepting the good and undermining his right to return or seek compensation. However, if the buyer does not affirm, i.e., continually lets the garage know that there has been problems, then he is not affirming the contract and will be entitled to a refund.

Be very careful here. Always assert your right, do not be afraid of complaining and keep a record of the number of times that you have complained.

Use of materials when carrying out repairs

Responsibility, or liability, for parts under a contract which is for works and materials is regulated by sections 3 and 4 of part 1 of the Supply of Goods and Services Act 1973. If a remedy is needed for the supply of parts which are either defective or are not those which are supposed to have been used then it is to this Act that you must turn. As before, the notion of affirmation and acceptance is of paramount importance.

When it comes to the service element of a contract, as opposed to the materials element, then it is to section 13 of the Supply of Goods and Services that you must turn. Section 13 states that work must be carried out with reasonable care and skill.

There is one famous legal case which tends to set the standard in this area. This case was Bolam v Friern Hospital in 1957. This involved the medical profession and the issue was deciding whether a doctor is liable for negligence and comparisons with a so-called "average doctor". The connection here is that if you are complaining about standards of work then you would need to demonstrate that the average garage could have carried out the work to a higher standard. There are other terms implied into a service contract. Section 14 implies that the business doing the servicing must carry it out within a

25

reasonable time. This is where there are no express terms in the agreement. Section 15 indicates that where no price has been agreed then a reasonable price must be agreed. A reasonable price is one which another company would charge for the same work.

Therefore, if you feel that you are being overcharged then you can challenge it, underpinned by the backing of section 15 of this Act. There is one very important rider here. That is if the supplier has quoted a high price and the consumer has accepted then there can be no redress, not even if you find that another company will provide that service for far less.

CONSUMER BEWARE. Always shop around. If you feel that the price is too high then ask elsewhere. Always try to avoid entering into an agreement with no stated price.

Of course, there will always be the case where it is not really possible to get a price. This is where protection under section 15 comes in.

EXAMPLE

You discover that you are receiving electric shocks off your car. You telephone a local garage that specialises in car electric's and the owner tells you to "drop your car in". You do this and telephone the garage later to see what the problem is. The garage owner informs you that the problem was minor, with a power lead earthing. The problem has been rectified and you can collect the car. You do this and you are informed that the bill is £150. Quite rightly, you think that this is too high. Two things can happen here, and often do. On one hand the garage owner can tell you that that is what he charges and you must pay it. The other is that you can find out what an alternative garage would pay for the same work and establish a reasonable price, refusing to go above this.

The problem that you have to sort out here is how to get your car back. You have to argue the case with the garage and let them know that you understand your rights as a consumer and you have read and understood the law that governs this particular problem.

It is the case that when businesses realise that they may get bad publicity and the person in front of them knows their rights, they generally back down, as it is bad for business. If there has been a breach of services contract then the normal solution or remedy is damages to put the defective or poor work right. Damages for distress or disappointment can be awarded in some cases although there are certain areas where it is difficult, such as holidays.

The Consumer Protection Act 1987

The above Act covers those instances where a person has been injured because of a defective good. This Act also covers the many instances where someone may have been injured or affected who is not the principal purchaser but has been injured.

The Consumer Protection Act therefore imposes a very strict liability for defective goods on someone who is deemed to be the producer of the product. The Act provides, or at least seeks to provide, a route for the consumer to seek redress against the person who is ultimately responsible for the damage. This gets rid, or at least minimises the requirement to have to prove fault, which in the past has proven very time consuming and difficult and also very expensive.

The Act is only relevant where the consumer has purchased a defective product which has caused damage. It is essential to determine who is liable, and the Act says that the following are primarily liable for damages:
a) the producer
b) an own brander who has held himself to be the producer of a particular good
c) the first importer into the European Community. Therefore, strict liability will attach to any person or company who presents its/his self as producer of a good.

Only in a few cases will the supplier of a good be liable. These cases are limited to instances where it may not be possible to identify the producer or anyone else within or further up the chain, in a reasonable period of time.

It is necessary to define product. This is because some goods and services are more readily identifiable than others as products. Section 1(2) of the Act defines product and has wide definitions. For example, goods include electricity. Section 45 also defines goods produced from the land, such as crops, and other goods such as aircraft vehicles etc. A product, however, is a common sense notion and for the purposes of the every day consumer a product is fairly obvious.

A defective product is simply where the safety of the product is in question and can be a manufacturing defect, a design defect and a defect that has arisen because of a misleading warning notice. In this latter instance, this means a notice that has failed to advise the consumer how to use a product properly.

A consumer can sue under the Consumer Protection Act (s5) for:

- Death caused as a result of a defective product
- Personal injury caused as a result of a defective product
- Damage to private property, above a certain sum, caused as a result of a defective product.

The is no liability for any damage to the product itself or for the loss of, or any damage to, the whole or any part of any product which has been supplied with a product.

There are cases where, even if a manufacturer is liable under the Act, the Act contains what is known as strict liability and not absolute liability. This means that there are a number of defences that can be used by manufacturers. It is up to the defendant, i.e., the manufacturer to prove one of the following as a defence:

- The defect was caused by the need to comply with the law as it stands at that time. This may have been the need to comply with new legislation that has recently been introduced
- The manufacturer did not supply the product in question-this can relate to instances of theft
- That the supplier of the good is not in business and is a private individual. Remember, the aim of the Act is to impose strict liability on commercial producers and it is not really the intention, or the spirit of the Act to impose any liability on individuals as such. However, individuals who are not in business are not ruled out.
- That the defect did not exist in the product at the time of supply. One very good example has been the recent spate of contaminating certain products as they lay on shelves, such a baby food and also chocolate. If contamination takes place in the shop then it is important to note that the seller, or retailer becomes liable under the Sale of Goods Act.

Another defence, perhaps the most complicated and controversial is that of the state of scientific (and technical) knowledge at the time was not such that a producer of products of the same description as the product in question might be expected to have discovered. Here, a producer of a product has to demonstrate that at the time in question they could not be expected to know of the defect. Finally, that the producer of a component part of a product had produced a defective product and the defect was as a result of instructions given by the main producer.

A consumer may bring a claim against a manufacturer within a certain timescale - in relation to personal injuries or any damage to property there is a three year time period within which to bring a claim. However, as far as a manufacturer of a product is concerned, there is a 10-year cut off point from the time that a particular product was supplied to a retailer.

There are some instances where a recall notice may be issued by a manufacturer to a retailer. This is happening all the time, in the cases of bay food, cars and other items. This in no way relieves the manufacturer of liability although it can certainly help to reduce the amount of compensation gained by an aggrieved person.

****

Chapter 4
Guarantees and Warranties

In the previous chapter we looked at defective goods and consumer remedies. In this chapter we will concentrate on the situation concerning guarantees and warranties issued by manufacturers.

A guarantee is most often issued by the manufacture of goods such as electrical goods, or by a company providing services such as replacement windows. It is normally provided free of charge when you buy the good or service. A guarantee usually offers to carry out repairs or make a replacement in the event of a fault arising.

Warranties

A warranty provides the same sort of cover that a guarantee does, but often you have to pay extra for it – for example many electrical stores provide warranties for five years, at a cost. These sorts of warranties are, effectively, insurance policies.

Legal protection with guarantees and warranties

A free guarantee for goods, including goods supplied with a service, is legally binding on the person offering the guarantee if the goods were bought on or after the 31st March 2003 (Sale and Supply of Goods to Consumers Regulations 2002). Guarantees issued before that date are not. A guarantee issued before 31st March 2003 will only be binding if you can show that it is part of your contract with the supplier of the goods or services or with the manufacturer. To be part of your contract, the terms of the guarantee must have been clearly set out when you bought the goods or services. Some firms supplying services offer ten-year guarantees or longer. These are of little value unless they are backed by an insurance company as they depend on the firm continuing in business.

The situation is similar with a warranty or extended guarantee. This is because you will have usually paid for it. This will then change the status of a warranty from a mere promise to do something, into a contractual obligation, which is enforceable in law. If a company does not honour a warranty then they can be sued.

Before agreeing to buy an extended guarantee or warranty you should look at:

- What is covered by the guarantee. Some extended guarantees or warranties will only cover mechanical breakdown and not wear or tear. Some will require you to pay labour charges.
- Whether the extended guarantee or warranty is underwritten by an insurance company. If the supplier goes out of business, you should still be able to claim from the underwriters for any work
- When the extended guarantee or warranty starts. You may find that your existing rights are sufficient anyway.
- If the goods or services are likely to have a considerable amount of use, it may be worth considering purchasing an extended guarantee or warranty.
- Whether you are already covered by your home contents insurance.
- Whether it would be cheaper to take out a separate insurance policy to cover several items.

Extended warranties for electrical goods
You have additional rights when you buy an extended warranty to cover domestic electrical goods. Traders must:

- Display the price of the warranty alongside the goods
- Give you a written quotation on request for the price of the warranty. They are legally obliged to honour the price if you go back within 30 days to buy the warranty after you have bought the goods
- Inform you of your rights to buy a warranty elsewhere and that the electrical item you bought may already be covered by your own household contents insurance.

You have the right to cancel the warranty within 45 days and get a full refund if you have not made a claim. If you make a claim on a warranty, you can still cancel and get a pro-rata refund at any time up until the end of the service agreement.

Frequent problems

Fridge freezer purchased 13 months ago and the fridge section has completely failed.

When you buy goods from a shop, you enter into a contract under the Sale of Goods Act 1979 which holds the shop liable for up to six years after purchase, providing that you can demonstrate that the problem is down to an unreasonable fault and not wear and tear. The guarantee issue is not relevant here. That is merely a promise by the manufacturer.

Damp proofing course carried out 5 years ago by a limited company, but noticed rising damp once again. Company claims that it was taken over by new owners and refuses to honour the original 10-year guarantee.

Your contract was with the original company and you cannot enforce the contract or any guarantees. Insurance does exist new for this type of problem

Read any guarantees or warranties carefully – get them in writing!

Chapter 5
Denying Liability For products

In the last chapter, we looked at guarantees and warranties and the rights and obligations of the consumer. In this chapter we will look at attempts to exclude or deny liability for a product.

We have all seen notices on products which say that the manufacturer is excluded from all liability for a good. This is a very important area and we need to look at the actual liability of a manufacturer even if an exclusion notice has been given. There is nothing stopping a shopkeeper or manufacturer from stonewalling your claim for damages due to the fact that an exclusion notice has been attached to a product.

Typical exclusion notices might read:

"No responsibility will be accepted for goods once they have left the store"
"There will be no refund for this good, even if found to be unsuitable"
"We accept no returns under any circumstances"

The list is endless and can apply to a whole range of products. However, what the consumer needs to know is whether a retailer can actually impose any of these restrictions. Can a retailer avoid the liabilities imposed under the Sale of Goods Act or the Supply of Goods Act or any other Act?

There is one major starting point for all exclusion notices. What we need to determine is whether or not the notice has been incorporated, or is an integral part of, the contract for sale. If this has not occurred then there can be no exclusion notice. Incorporation means that if a consumer signs a contract they are bound by it, in the absence of any sort of misrepresentation. So, if a consumer has signed a contract they are bound by its terms. However, if the terms contained in an unsigned document which is an exclusion notice, the terms will only form part of the actual contract if there has been an attempt to bring the notice to the consumers attention.

The Unfair Contract Terms Act 1977 is of importance in determining whether or not a consumer has signed an unfair, or onerous contract. The Act will govern any clause which purports or attempts to restrict liability. The Act governs business and will control the acts of a person who, through contract, attempts to deny any liability for a good where, in fact, there does exist a liability in law.

If we look at the matter objectively, as we have seen so far there are a range of laws which protect the consumer and place obligations on manufacturers and suppliers. Merely to insert an exclusion clause, thereby giving full protection against the law, is an absurdity.

In practice, the unfair Contract Terms Act operates in three areas:
- Where there are exclusions in relation to the implied terms section of the Sale of Goods Act 1979 and the 1982 Sale of Goods Act (implied Terms).
- The person supplying the goods is trying to avoid negligence based liability;
- The person supplying the goods is trying to avoid liability for any other breach of contract.

Example A removal firm undertakes to do a job for Mr and Mrs Smith. They inform the couple that their liability for any damages to goods is covered by an exclusion clause in a contract that they wish to sign. This states that liability for any damage is limited to £35 per item or £100 in total.

Can they do this? What they are trying to do is to avoid the above Acts which impose liabilities for negligence and the answer would be no, they cannot limit there own liability.

A very important point to note is that if you are dealing with a retailer as a consumer then the retailer cannot avoid responsibility as contained in the implied terms of contract which are governed by the Sale of Goods and Supply of Goods Acts.

There may be occasions where other goods, such as exchanged goods, hire goods or the materials part of a contract are concerned and the Supply of Goods Act (implied terms) and Sale of Goods Act do not apply. The Supply of Goods and Services Act governs these areas and section seven of the Unfair Contract Terms Act refers.

The Unfair Contract Terms Act also covers negligence based clauses, i.e., where a manufacturer denies liability for negligence. Section 1 of the UCTA defines negligence as the breach of duty of care arising in contract.

As far as the consumer is concerned, the area which is most likely to arise is an attempt to avoid liability for a breach of section 13 of the Supply of Goods and Services Act.

Section 2 of the Unfair Contract Terms Act says that any clause (or notice) is invalid insofar as it attempts to exclude liability for negligence *resulting in death or personal injury.*

Section 2(2) of the Act also goes on to state that if any other loss or damage arises as a result then the clause of the notice will only be valid provided a reasonableness test is satisfied. The reasonableness test contains guidelines and include:

a) the strength of the bargaining position between parties to a contract
b) whether there was any inducement to agree to the term, i.e., was there any special offer or was the consumer put in a position where he/ she had to agree before purchase;
c) whether the consumer knew of any term in the first place;
d) whether the goods were specially manufactured.

The Unfair Contract Terms Act also deals with other breaches of contract such as where a business will try to exclude or restrict liability to a certain sum or claims to be entitled to give a good or service which is in fact substantially different to that stated. A common example here is that of a tour operator stating that they have the right to offer alternative holidays. The UCTA also covers the notice which claims to have no liability for the non delivery of a service.

Section 4 of the Act states that a person dealing as a consumer cannot be made to indemnify another person against liability for negligence or breach of contract unless the reasonableness test has been passed. Section 5 deals with manufacturers guarantees to the consumer and states that if goods which are supplied for private use or consumption prove defective whilst in use and cause loss or damage as a result of negligence in manufacture or distribution, then any attempt to avoid liability in a guarantee is void.

If misrepresentation is involved, then any attempt to exclude liability for misrepresentation is only valid provided that the reasonableness test is passed.

There are areas of law which will make it a criminal liability to give an exclusion notice. The Consumer Transactions (Restrictions on Statements) Order 1976 as amended, makes it a criminal offence to use a void exemption clause in a contract. Therefore, a notice such as no refunds etc., can make the seller criminally liable. The order also makes it an offence to supply goods to a consumer with written exclusion notices without pointing out that a consumers statutory rights are unaffected.

The effect of the European Community and European Directives.

There are attempts to make liability for consumer goods standard throughout the European Community and there is a European Directive on unfair terms in Consumer contracts which will seek to give the consumer more power, particularly when dealing with large companies or

37

corporations. Contracts which operate to the detriment of the consumer will not be allowed. The draft directive is concerned only with contracts between business and consumers. No contracts will be excluded from the directive.

****

Chapter 6

Unsolicited Goods

Unsolicited goods are those which are sent to a person without their requesting them. This has caused problems for consumers where delivery was inevitably followed by aggressive sales tactics, such as sending an invoice for a price. This problem was originally overcome by the Unsolicited Goods and Services Act 1971 which gave protection in both civil law and criminal law.

Civil Law

The civil law (previously covered by the Unsolicited Goods and Services Act 1971) is now covered by the Consumer Protection (Distance Selling) Regulations 2000. Regulation 24 applies where:

- unsolicited goods are sent to a person with a view to his acquiring them; and
- the recipient has no reasonable cause to believe that they were sent with a view to their being acquired for the purpose of business and the recipient has not agreed to acquire the goods or to return them.

Where these conditions are fulfilled, regulation 24(2) provides that, as between the recipient and the sender, the recipient may use, deal with or dispose of the goods as if they were an absolute gift.

The regulations also provide that the rights of the sender to the goods are extinguished. These regulations are stricter than the previous law, where recipients could not dispose of the goods right away but had to retain them for a certain time first.

Criminal law

If you receive a demand for payment for unsolicited goods or services, you can ignore it. If the trader does this, they may have committed a criminal offence under the Consumer Protection from Unfair Trading Regulations 2008 (see Chapter 11). You should report the matter to your trading standards department through Citizens Advice.

It is also an offence to:

- assert a right to payment; or
- threaten to bring legal proceedings in respect of the goods; or
- place or threaten to place the name of any person on a defaulter list; or
- invoke or threaten to invoke any other collection procedure.

****

Chapter 7

Purchasing Goods at Home

In the previous chapter, we looked at consumer rights when a manufacturer attempts to deny or to exclude liability. In this chapter we will look at consumer rights when buying goods at home, on the doorstep and, in particular, at The Distance Selling Regulations 2000.

Buying on the doorstep

If you buy goods or services from a trader who visits your home, for example from a door-to-door salesperson, or from a party plan event, the law says that the goods must:

- match their description-this means they must be as described by the seller and in accordance with any packaging descriptions
- be of satisfactory quality-this means the goods meet the standards that any reasonable person would expect, taking into account the description, price and all other relevant information. The goods must also be fit for purpose.

If you make an agreement to have a service carried out, for example, agree to have building work undertaken, the law says that the work must be carried out with reasonable care and skill, finished in a reasonable time and provided at a reasonable cost.

Criminal offences

It is a criminal offence for a trader to sell you goods which are unsafe, do not match their description or which have been advertised at a misleading price. This is not the case, however, if the goods were purchased from a private individual. If you have any problems and think that an offence may have been committed you should report the matter to Citizens Advice Consumer Helpline on 08454 04 05 05. If you have used your credit card or the seller introduced you to finance to pay for the goods or services, and the cost of the goods or services is between £100 and £30,000, the credit company may be equally liable for any breach of contract, for example if the goods are faulty.

Cancelling an agreement

If you decide that you don't want the goods or services you have a right in certain circumstances to cancel the agreement as long as you do so in seven days, known as the cooling off period (as mentioned in the introduction, under the new draft Consumer Rights Bill, it is proposed that this be extended to 14 days). If you cancel during this period then you are entitled to your money back, although if some work has been carried out then there will be a charge usually for this work. The trader should give you written cancellation rights when the contract is formed.

You do not have the right to cancel certain agreements where:

- the goods or services you bought were less than £35, unless you signed a credit agreement at home in which case you can cancel the agreement regardless of amount paid; or
- you contacted the seller and asked them to visit you; or
- the service included new building works, such as a conservatory; or
- you bought food and other perishable goods; or

- you bought goods from a home party sale. However, if you were invited to a friends house without knowing that there were goods for sale there, you then have the right to cancel.

Cancelling a credit agreement made at home

There are different rules in force for cancelling when a credit agreement is signed at home. If you sign a credit agreement in your home for more than £35, after a face-to-face discussion with the seller then you are entitled to a cooling off period. After signing the agreement, you should be given a copy of the credit agreement clearly setting out your cancellation rights. You should also receive by post a second notification of your cancellation rights. The cooling off period begins on the day you sign the agreement and ends five days after you have received the second notification of your cancellation rights. If you wish to cancel the credit agreement you should write to the credit company involved without delay. Keep a copy of the letter, having sent it by recorded delivery.

Faulty goods or services

The question of whether you can get a refund depends on when you reported the fault and what type of contract that you have, whether for goods or services. In the case of goods, it stands to reason that the less time that you have had them and the quicker that you report the problem the more chance that you have of getting the money back. If you keep the goods for a while you may have lost the right to a refund but may be entitled to a replacement or repair. This very much depends on the circumstances of the purchase.

In the case of services, if the work has not commenced and the trader is in breach of the contract signed with you, you should be entitled to get back any money paid to date. If the work has started but has been shoddily carried out then you may be entitled to compensation, after you have tried to get the trader to rectify the problem. There are a number of situations where you may be entitled to compensation:

- breach of contract
- dangerous or unsafe work
- the seller has repaired the goods but the repair is unsatisfactory
- false statements have been made about the goods
- additional expenses have been incurred because of faulty workmanship.

It will be the seller, and not the manufacturer who will be liable for the problem, and responsible for solving it. You should stop using the goods in question and contact the seller and the credit company as soon as possible after discovering the fault or problem. If you have difficulty finding out the address or telephone number of the seller then you should contact the Direct Selling Association (DSA) on 01604 625700. They are concerned with all types of agreements made in the home. They will provide you with invaluable advice.

Distance Selling

Many people buy goods using the internet or fax, or from home shopping on the TV, or from catalogues. The law recognises that this type of shopping comes with its own type of problems. For example, what happens if the goods do not turn up or you don't like them once you have received them? People who shop at home have rights under the Consumer Protection (Distance Selling) Regulations 2000.

Briefly, these Regulations say that you should be given clear information about the order and the company, along with a cooling off period, and protection against credit card fraud and the menace of unsolicited goods.

What isn't covered by these regulations?

- Financial services like banking and insurance
- Auctions
- Goods bought from a vending machine
- Goods bought using a payphone
- Contracts for the sale of land
- Food and drink, or other goods for everyday consumption delivered by rounds men
- Accommodation, transport, catering and leisure facilities for a specific time or date
- Timeshare and package holidays
- The regulations only apply when you buy from a trader who is organised to sell to you without face-to-face contact. So, if you saw something in a shop, went home and bought by phone, this is not distance selling.

The right to clear information

Before you decide to buy, the seller must give you the following information:

- The name of the trader, along with their postal address if you have to pay in advance
- An accurate description of the goods and services
- The price, along with any taxes or delivery charges if relevant and how long the price or offer remains valid
- Delivery arrangements, which should be within 30 days unless agreed otherwise
- Payment arrangements
- The right to cancel the order

- Information about whether you will be liable for the cost of returning the goods if you change your mind
- For services provided over a period of time, such as a mobile phone contract, or a gas supply contract, you must be told what the duration of that contract will be

After you buy, the trader must provide you with the following information:

- Written confirmation of your order (by letter, e-mail or fax) including the information outlined above, if not already provided
- Written information on how to cancel, a contact postal address and details of any guarantees, warranties or after sales service
- Details of how and when to end a contract for the provision of a service if there is no specified finish date
- This information should be sent to you by the time the goods are delivered.

Your right to cancel

The Distance Selling Regulations 2000 give you the right to change your mind and cancel an order within seven working days (to be extended to 14 days under the draft Consumer Rights Bill). If you do decide to cancel, then you should put this in writing, either by letter or you can fax or e-mail. The time limits are:

- For goods – seven working days after the day on which the goods are received
- For services – seven working days after the day on which you agreed to go ahead with the agreement

What isn't covered by this cooling off period?

- Services that are to be provided within seven working days. If you have agreed that the service will be provided before the end of the cooling off period you will not be entitled to cancel once the service has started, but the trader must tell you this in writing.

- Goods made to your personal requirements or specifications
- Goods which may deteriorate quickly, such as flowers or food
- Sealed audio or video recordings or computer software that have been opened.
- Betting, gaming or lottery services
- Newspapers, periodicals or magazines.
- Internet, television or some other distance selling outlet are covered by the Consumer protection (Distance Selling) Regulations 2000
- There are a number of items not covered by the above regulations
- There is a right to clear information from distance selling traders
- There is a clear right to cancel a purchase

If the seller is based outside of the UK

If the seller is based outside of the UK, but in another member country of the European Union, the situation can be slightly more complicated. You may, because it is an EU country, have the same or similar rights to those you have in the UK. If the seller is based outside of the EU, your rights will depend on the laws of that country.

If goods don't arrive

If the goods aren't delivered by the agreed date or within thirty days, you have the right to either cancel the order and get your money back or ask for a replacement.

If you have paid for the goods in advance and the seller has gone out of business, you might be able to get a refund if the seller is a member of the Safe Home Ordering Protection Scheme (SHOPS) or the Periodical Publishers Association (PPA) schemes. If you paid by credit card and the trader introduced you to a credit deal, and the goods cost more than £100 and less than £30,000 the company who provided the credit will be liable equally for any breach of contract.

There are a number of organisations that deal with complaints about mail order companies: The Mail Order Traders Association; The Direct Marketing Association and the Advertising Standards Authority. You should refer to the useful addresses at the back of this book.

****

Chapter 8

Consumers and Credit

In the previous chapter we looked at the law concerning buying goods at home, in particular the Distance Selling Regulations 2000, which have greatly strengthened consumer rights. In this chapter we will look at the all-important area of consumer credit.

At the time of writing the Government has tightened up on the laws governing Consumer credit, specifically the area of credit cards, which they see as out of control, leading to unacceptable levels of consumer debt. The area of payday loans is also being looked at, with a view to capping loans, in the light of exorbitant interest rates (see chapter 16, Consumer Issues Generally). Also, for more details on payday loans and regulation you should contact one of the consumer organisations listed in the back of this book.

The most important Act dealing with consumers and credit is the Consumer Credit Act 1974. This act also encompasses loans from pawnbrokers and also payday loans. This has been supplemented by the Consumer Credit (Advertising) Regulations 2011 (see further on in this chapter).

Nowadays, many people use credit to help them with their buying. It helps to spread the load, especially with expensive items such as furniture or cars. But borrowing can be costly and with so many different types of credit available, it is wise to shop around before you sign any credit agreement.

Using a credit card when buying a single item costing over £100 but under £30,000 can provide extra protection if you have a problem with your purchase. Whether you use your credit card to pay the full amount or even part of the deposit (as little as £1 but no more than £25,000), the credit card company is legally bound to help in cases of faulty goods or non-delivery if the retailer goes out of business.

Try to avoid interest charges by paying your credit card bill off in full when it arrives. Be warned, however, that you may not be protected if your payment is made through a third party - see the section below on credit cards.

What the law says

The main law to give you protection when buying on credit is the Consumer Credit Act 1974. By law you're entitled to a copy of your credit agreement so make sure you get one. Never sign a blank form or even leave some sections blank.

Right of withdrawal

You have a right to withdraw from a credit agreement without giving any reason, within 14 days. When the 14 day period begins will depend on when the agreement is made and there must be information in the agreement telling you about your withdrawal rights. On withdrawal you must repay the amount of money received and any interest accrued.

Credit cards

Under section 75 of the Consumer Credit Act 1974, if you use your credit card to buy a single item costing more than £100 but no more than £30,000, you can claim from the credit card company or the trader if something goes wrong. Many websites use an online payment processor such as Paypal, Worldpay or Google Checkout. While the law in this area is not certain, you may not be covered by the protection offered by section 75. Online payment processors do have their own refund systems, so make sure you read their terms and conditions carefully. If you use a credit card to buy airline or other travel tickets from a travel agent you cannot normally claim against the travel agent if the airline delays or cancels the flight as they were contracted to supply the ticket, not the flight. However, if you use a credit card to buy the travel agent's own package of travel arrangements the agent then becomes the supplier of the holiday package and has equal liability with the credit card company.

Credit reference agencies

You don't have a right to credit. Before giving you credit, lenders want to check whether you're an acceptable risk. To help them do this they may check with firms called Credit Reference Agencies (CRAs). These agencies don't keep 'black lists' or give an opinion as to whether or not you should be given credit. They just provide information about your credit record. You are entitled to see a copy of any information they hold on you and to correct anything in it that you can prove is wrong. You are entitled to see a copy of your file if you make a written request and send £2. Online and telephone requests may cost more. The contact details of the credit reference agencies are shown below and you can also find more information on the website of the Money Advice Service. The CRA commits a criminal offence if it fails to correct files.

Credit unions

To borrow from a credit union you must first become a member and show by saving regularly over a set period that you will be able to afford the repayments. This is an excellent way of getting credit as the interest rate is usually lower than that used by other lenders.

Hire purchase

You cannot end a hire purchase agreement unless you are up to date with your payments. You will have to pay at least half of the total hire purchase price. You cannot sell the goods until the agreement has been paid off.

Logbook loans

Consumers will regularly see these loans being advertised on the high street or on the internet promising cash fast, but they can often prove to be more problematic than beneficial for borrowers. A logbook loan is a loan secured on your vehicle. You will be asked to hand over the logbook (V5 form - vehicle registration document) and sign a document called a bill of sale. This means that the protection provided by the Consumer Credit Act – that cars cannot be seized without a court order – is removed and the lender can then seize the car if the loan is not paid.

The bill of sale also transfers temporary ownership of your vehicle to the lender, but you are still able to use it while you are making the loan repayments. You only become the legal owner of the vehicle once again when you have settled the agreement in full.

Consumers should consider other types of borrowing before agreeing to a logbook loan, especially if you cannot do without your vehicle. Although these loans provide quick access to money, the APR is likely to be very high, commonly over 200% APR. There may be cheaper ways you can borrow, which do not put you at such a risk of losing your assets. The concept of a logbook loan can be complicated, so if you plan to take one out make sure you ask the lender to explain anything you do not understand. It is vitally important you understand your responsibilities under the agreement to help you minimise the risk of losing your vehicle.

Furthermore, the law only recognises the bill of sale if the lender registers it with the High Court. If it is not registered, the lender must get a court's approval to repossess your vehicle. So if you think you may fall behind with your loan repayments and want to know what will happen to your vehicle, you will need to check if the bill of sale is registered. You will need to give both your and your lender's name and address along with a small fee to the High Court.

Money lenders

They charge high interest rates and you should be very careful with this type of credit. Avoid anyone who simply calls at your home or speaks to you in the pub and offers you a loan: they are committing a criminal offence. Money leaders may ask for some security for the loan. If they do, never give them your child benefit book or other social security book.

Payday loans

Consumers unable to access credit through traditional banking means are increasingly turning to alternative sources, including payday loan companies. Payday, or paycheque loans, are short-term loans that you get in return for your pay cheque or proof of your income. They are basically cash advances on the salary you are expecting and are available online and on the high street.

They can be a way of getting your hands on your wages quicker than you otherwise would, but it is important to be aware of the high interest rates charged and the consequences of falling behind with your repayment.

This type of borrowing is not suitable for those looking to repay their loans over a long period, as they are designed to be short-term loans to deal with short-term personal cash flow issues. If loans are rolled over, debts could escalate and consumers could get into difficulties. They should only be considered if consumers are confident that they'll be able to repay the debt in full when it is due.

If you are considering using a payday loan company, you should look into all the available alternatives first:

- Speak to your bank manager as you may be able to get an agreed overdraft

- Look into Social Fund Loans - these are government-funded, interest-free loans available to those on low incomes

- Check out your local credit union.

If you have no alternative to a payday loan make sure:

- You fully understand the costs and charges involved as rates higher than 1,000% APR are common

- You do not borrow more than you can repay or for longer than necessary. If you miss the repayment, the cost of borrowing even a small amount can become very high, very quickly

- The lender is licensed by the Office of Fair Trading.

If consumers find themselves relying on payday loans regularly they may find it useful to re-examine their household budget.

Personal loans

Shop around for the best value. Always consider how long it will take you to pay back the loan and how much you will pay in total, as well as how much your monthly payments are. Always check the Annual Percentage Rate (APR) being charged. It is the best way of comparing one deal with another. Generally, the lower the APR, the better the deal.

What to do if you have a complaint

Even if you think the goods are faulty, don't stop your payments or you could end up in trouble. See the shop manager at once and let your finance company know about the problem. If you can't sort it out yourself you should ask for advice from Consumerline on 0300 123 6262, your local Advice Centre or Citizens Advice. You can also get debt advice from the agencies shown below.

If at any stage you feel that the lender is generally trading unfairly, the matter can be referred to the Office of Fair Trading which issues credit licences to all authorised lenders.

The Consumer Credit (Advertisements) Regulations

The Consumer Credit (Advertisements) Regulations 2010 (SI 2010/1970) were laid before Parliament on 5 August 2010, and came into force on 1 February 2011. The Regulations extend to all forms of advertising, including in print, on television or radio, on the internet or by way of telephone canvassing. Certain advertisements indicate that the credit is available only to bodies corporate or only for business purposes.

Representative examples

- Where an advertisement contains an interest rate, which will include a reference to 0% credit, or any figure relating to the cost of credit, then a "representative example" must be given within the advertisement. It will therefore no longer be possible to quote an interest rate within an advertisement without triggering the requirement to display a representative example.

- The standard information to be included in a representative example comprises:

    o the total amount of credit;

    o the rate of interest, and whether that rate is fixed or variable;

    o the nature and amount of any charge included in the total charge for credit;

    o the representative APR (except in advertisements for authorised non-business overdrafts);

    o the cash price of goods and any advance payment (where appropriate); and o unless the agreement is open ended, the length of the agreement, the total amount payable and the amount of each repayment of credit (where appropriate).

Note that other rates of interest and charges may be included in the advertisement, but these must be separate from the representative example and less prominent.

- The official guidance issued by BIS in relation to the new Regulations in August 2010 states that where the credit agreement provides for interest to be compounded, then the equivalent annual rate ("EAR") of interest should be shown, rather than a simple rate of interest.

- The representative APR should be denoted as "%APR", accompanied by the word "representative" and where the APR is subject to change be accompanied by the word "variable".

- The Regulations provide that a "representative APR" is the APR at, or below, which the advertiser reasonably expects credit to be provided under at least 51% of the consumer credit agreements entered into as a result of the advertisement. This differs from the current typical APR requirement which is based on the highest APR that at least 66% of the borrowers accepting credit as a result of the advertisement are given.

- The Regulations require all the standard information to be set out in a clear and concise way and to be accompanied by the words "representative example". All the information should be presented together and must be given equal prominence. The information must be given greater prominence than any other information which triggers the inclusion of the representative APR, for example, the cost of the credit.

- Prominence requires the standard information to stand out from any other information relating to the cost of credit. It should be easily legible. The Regulations do not require any particular font size.

- In respect of running-account credit or where the amount of credit is not known, the representative APR should be based on £1200 (or where the credit is definitely less than that amount, an amount equal to the limit).

- Other than in certain limited circumstances, such as radio or TV advertisements, or those on the premises of the creditor, the advertisement must specify a postal address at which the advertiser may be contacted.

Indicators and incentives

- There are some circumstances where a representative example is not required, other than general advertising with no interest rates or indications of cost. Where an advertisement contains either:

  o indicators that credit is available to "non-status" borrowers, or

  o comparative indicators that credit is available on more favourable terms than credit offered by the advertiser or other credit providers, or

  o includes incentives to apply for credit

then, **_provided_** that the advertisement states the representative APR and no other interest rate or amount relating to the cost of credit, it does not need to include the standard information by way of a representative example, nor a postal address for the advertiser. The representative APR in this instance must be of greater prominence than the indicators or incentives.

Security

- Any credit advertisement that requires security to be granted must specify that security is or may be required and must state the nature of that security. Unlike the 2004 Regulations no wording is prescribed for this and there are no requirements concerning prominence. The information must however be clear and easily legible.

Restrictions on certain expressions

- The Regulations retain other features of the existing UK advertising regime, such as restrictions on the use of certain expressions, for example, "overdraft", "interest free", "loan guaranteed", "gift" etc, other than where these expressions are appropriate given the nature of the credit on offer.

Commencement and transitional arrangements

- The 2010 Advertisement Regulations came into force on 1 February 2011. They apply to credit advertisements published on or after 1 February 2011, or which continue to be published after that date, subject to some limited transitional provisions.

Breach

- Breach of the Regulations is an offence, and persistent breaches may be considered by the OFT when it considers any application to renew a consumer credit license.

Credit agencies in the UK

There are three main credit agencies in the UK. They are:

Callcredit Check
PO Box 734
Leeds
LS1 9GX
www.callcreditcheck.com

Experian Limited
Landmark House
Experian Way
NG2 Business Park
Nottingham NG80 1ZZ
Tel: 0844 481 8000

Equifax plc
PO Box 1140
Bradford
BD1 5US
www.equifax.co.uk

You can write to the above any time and ask to see the information they have on you. You can also order your file online and over the telephone from Equifax and Experion so long as you have a credit or debit card in your own name.

If you write you will need to send a fee, usually £25, give full name address and date of birth, include any other address that you have had within the last six years, give your business name and address if you are a sole trader or partnership. Keep copies of any letters that you send. The agency must reply within seven working days to ask for any more information from you, tell you that it does not have a file on you or send you the file.

If a lender or other turns you down for a loan, you can check the information that has been provided. You can ask for the name of the credit reference agency that provided information about you if:

- You write to the lender within 28 days of your last contact about the credit deal
- The lender used a credit agency, they must tell you the agency's name and address within seven working days of your letter.

There are several organisations that will assist if you have a specific complaint against a lender. they are listed below.

The Consumer Credit Association (CCA)

The CCA represents over 75% of firms that provide unsecured loans in the home credit industry. The CCA has a code of practice which its members must comply with, as well as a business conduct pledge. The CCA also has internal conciliation and arbitration schemes to help resolve complaints made against its members. they can be contacted as follows:

CCA
Queens House
Queens Road
Chester
CH1 3BQ

Tel: 01244 312044
Fax: 01244 318035

email: complaints@ccauk.org
Website: www.ccauk.org

Consumer Credit Trade Association (CCTA)

The CCTA represents credit lenders including finance houses, retailers and building societies. The CCTA has a code of practice with which its members must comply. The CCTA has an internal conciliation scheme to resolve complaints made against its members. there is also an independent arbitration scheme, run by the Chartered Institute of Arbitrators. The CCTA can be contacted as follows:

CCTA
Suite 4
The Wave
1 View Croft Road
Shipley
West Yorkshire
BD17 7DU

Tel: 01274 714959
Fax: 0845 257 1199
email: info@ccta.co.uk
Website: www.ccta.co.uk

The Finance and Leasing Association (FLA)

The FLA represents the UK and finance leasing industry, including creditors offering hire purchase and conditional sale agreements, secured and unsecured loans, credit cards and store cards. The FLA has a code of practice with which all its full members must comply. The FLA has an independent arbitration scheme for consumer complaints which is run by the Chartered Institute of Arbitrators. The contact details are as follows:

Finance and Leasing Association
2nd Floor Imperial House

15-19 Kingsway
London
WC2B 6UN

Tel: 020 7836 6511
fax 020 7420 9600
email: info@ fla.org.uk
Website: www.fla.org.uk

****

Chapter 9

Defective Goods Purchased on Credit

In the previous chapter, we looked at the position of the consumer when wishing to withdraw from an agreement. In this chapter we will look at the position of the consumer when purchasing goods on credit.

The consumers recourse to change of goods or money back will lie with whomever he/she has the agreement. We have seen that the business with whom the purchaser has the contract will be liable under the various Acts for defective goods.

Unable to meet repayments

The first action here should be for the consumer to try to reach an agreement with the creditor. The creditor, when making a decision will be influenced by a number of factors, such as the saleability of the goods. The type of credit agreement must be considered here. If the agreement is a loan the main principle is that it must be repaid. The only escape route, or breathing space for the debtor is that time to repay may be given.

If the agreement is a hire purchase or conditional sale agreement, then the finance company has legal title to the goods and one of the options open to the debtor who does not wish to keep the goods is to exercise his rights to terminate under section 99-100 of the Consumer Credit Act. This is a costly option. For termination to operate under section 99:
a) the agreement must be regulated under the Consumer Protection Act;
b) it is available at any time before the final payment becomes due;
c) all arrears must be paid;
d) the debtor is liable to pay the creditor half of the total price.

All of the above examples have been based on the fact that the consumer may wish to keep the goods. There may be a situation where the debtor might want to hang on to the goods. This also depends on the type of the credit agreement. If the agreement is a loan then it must be repaid. The goods purchased are the debtors and can be sold to repay the loan. If a debtor gets into any kind of financial difficulties then a default notice will be served on him by the finance company. This notice must be served before any further action can be taken. At least seven days must be given to remedy the breach. The debtor, in response can, if he wishes apply to the court for a time order. This gives more time to pay off arrears.

The debtor can also retain goods by making them "protected". This means, basically, that he finance company, or whoever owns the goods will have to obtain a court order before the goods can be seized. This take time and the debtor will gain longer to pay off debts owed. The Consumer Credit act also provides that goods are protected if the debtor has paid more than one third of the total price, the debtor is in breach of the agreement, the agreement is still valid and the property is owned by the creditor. If the creditor does seize the goods back without a court order, the agreement is terminated and the debtor can obtain all money paid to date as a refund.

The Consumer Credit Act and "Extortionate credit bargains"

This is a fairly new concept, having been introduced into the Consumer Credit Act in 1978. The extortionate credit bargains provisions apply even if the credit exceeds £15,000. The Act (s138) states that a bargain is extortionate if it requires the debtor to make payments which are grossly exorbitant. The concept of grossly exorbitant will take into account interest rates prevailing at the time of the transaction and also other factors such as the relationship of the creditor with the debtor. The debtor can take proceedings through the county court to have the bargain re-examined and reopened.

The position when purchasing hire goods

There has been a marked increase in the incidence of hired goods during the last ten years. This is partly to do with the cyclical nature of our economy and the fact that it is quite often cheaper to hire goods than to buy them. In addition, if a person needs an expensive good, such as a floor sander, for a few days only then it is obviously cheaper to rent than buy. The Sale of Goods Act does not cover hired items as there has been no transfer of goods. However, Part 1 of the 1982 Supply of Goods Act covers hired goods. Exclusion notices are covered by the Unfair Contract Terms Act, section 7. Section 101 0f the Supply of Goods Act 1982 governs the right of the hirer to terminate the agreement after 18 months, even if the hire period was longer. All money due within the 18 months must be paid

****

Chapter 10

The Consumer Protection from Unfair Trading Regulations 2008

Trade Descriptions-Misleading Prices-Aggressive Selling and General Unfair Practices

The Consumer Protection from Unfair Trading Regulations 2008 (known as the CPRs) cover commercial practices between traders and consumers - 'acts, omissions, course of conduct, representation or commercial communication (including advertising and marketing) by a trader, which is directly connected with the promotion, sale or supply of a product to or from consumers, whether occurring before, during or after a commercial transaction (if any) in relation to a product'. Note: a 'product' is any goods or service, and includes rights and obligations.

The legislation
The Consumer Protection from Unfair Trading Regulations 2008 came into force on 26 May 2008 and implement the European Union-wide Unfair Commercial Practices Directive (UCPD). The aim of the UCPD is to harmonise consumer protection laws across the European Union to prevent business practices that are unfair to consumers and all Member States are introducing equivalent legislation.

The Regulations replace a lot of consumer protection legislation, including Part III of the Consumer Protection Act 1987 (which dealt with misleading prices), the majority of the Trade Descriptions Act 1968, and the Control of Misleading Advertising Regulations 1988.

What is prohibited?

Effectively the CPRs prohibit trading practices that are unfair to consumers. There are four different types of practices to consider:

1.   Practices prohibited in all circumstances

2.   Misleading actions and omissions

3.   Aggressive practices

4.   General duty not to trade unfairly

For the last three practice types above it is necessary to show that the action of the trader has an effect (or is likely to have an effect) on the actions of the consumer. There does not have to be a physical consumer as this is a test looking at how the average consumer is - or is likely to be - affected.

The CPRs identify three different types of consumer:

- average consumer

- targeted consumer

- vulnerable consumer

...recognising that different types of consumers may react to a practice in different ways.

1. Practices prohibited in all circumstances

Schedule 1 to the CPRs (PDF 195KB) introduces 31 practices that are always considered to be unfair and therefore are banned in all circumstances. These include:

False endorsements/authorisation

- false claims of membership of trade associations

- claiming a product has been approved by a public or private body when it has not.

Misleading avaiability

- bait advertising (or 'bait and switch') where a trader lures a consumer into believing he can buy a product at a low price when the trader is aware he does not have reasonable stock available or is not able to supply at that price, or attempts to 'sell-up' to a higher priced product

- falsely stating a product is only available for a very limited time in order to make the consumer make an immediate decision

Misleading context/effect

- claiming a trader is going to cease trading or move premises when he is not (for example, bogus closing down sales)

- falsely claiming a product has curative properties

- describing a product as 'free', 'gratis', 'without charge' or similar if a consumer is going to have to pay more than the cost of responding to the advertisement and collecting or paying for delivery of the item

- including an invoice or similar in marketing material, implying a consumer has ordered the product when he has not

- failing to make it clear that a person is actually a trader or creating the impression he is a consumer (for example, failing to indicate trade status when selling a second-hand car)

- creating the impression that a product can legally be sold, when in fact, it cannot

Pyramid schemes

- operating or promoting such schemes are specifically prohibited, provided they fit within the definition of a pyramid scheme (that is, a scheme where a consumer gives consideration for the opportunity to receive compensation that is derived primarily from the introduction of other consumers into the scheme, rather than from the sale or consumption of products)

Prize draws

- competitions where the prizes described (or equivalent) are not awarded

- creating the false impression that a consumer has won, or will win, a prize when there is no prize or claiming the prize is subject to the consumer paying money or incurring a cost

Agressive sales

- creating the impression a consumer can't leave the premises until a contract is formed

- visiting a consumer at home and refusing to leave when asked to leave (except when the trader has a legal right to enforce a contractual obligation)

- making persistent and unwanted solicitations by phone/fax/email (except when a trader has a legal right to enforce a contractual obligation)

- making a direct exhortation to children to buy a product or to persuade their parents to buy a product for them (pester power)

- telling a consumer a trader's job will be in jeopardy if the consumer does not buy the product

Unreasonable demands

- requiring a consumer who wishes to claim on an insurance policy to produce irrelevant documents or failing to respond to correspondence in order to dissuade the consumer from exercising his contractual rights

2. Misleading actions and omissions

The CPRs prohibit misleading actions and misleading omissions that cause, or are likely to cause, the average consumer to take a different transactional decision - that is, any decision taken by the consumer concerning the purchasing of the product or whether to exercise a contractual right in relation to the product, including decisions not to act. This does not only relate to pre-shopping but includes after-sales and continues for the lifetime of the product.

MISLEADING ACTIONS (REGULATION 5)

This regulation prohibits giving false information to, or deceiving, consumers. A misleading action occurs when a practice misleads through the information it contains, or its deceptive presentation, and causes, or is likely to cause, the average consumer to take a different transactional decision.

There are three different types of misleading actions:

- misleading information generally (see below)

- creating confusion with competitors' products

- failing to honour commitments made in a code of conduct

The information that may be considered as misleading is very wide, and is listed in the legislation itself, including such things as:

- the existence or nature of the product

- the main characteristics of the product - for example, the benefits of the product or the geographical origin

- the price or the manner in which it is calculated

- the need for a service, part, replacement or repair

- the nature, attributes and rights of the trader - such as qualifications

MISLEADING OMISSIONS (REGULATION 6)

This regulation prohibits giving insufficient information about a product. It is a breach of the CPRs to fail to give consumers the information they need to make an informed choice in relation to a product if this would cause, or be likely to cause, the average consumer to take a different transactional decision.

A trader is required to give consumers material information, that is the information the average consumer needs, according to the context, to make an informed choice.

It is a breach of the CPRs:

- to omit material information

- to hide material information

- to provide material information in a manner that is unclear, unintelligible, ambiguous or untimely

- to fail to identify the commercial intent (unless this is apparent from the context)

3. Aggressive practices (regulation 7)

The CPRs prohibit aggressive commercial practices that intimidate or exploit consumers, restricting their ability to make free or informed choices. In order for an aggressive practice to be unfair it must cause, or be likely to cause, the average consumer to take a different transactional decision.

A commercial practice is aggressive if:

- it significantly impairs, or is likely to significantly impair, the average consumer's freedom of choice or conduct in relation to the product through the use of harassment, coercion or undue influence, and

- it thereby causes him to take a different transactional decision

To decide whether a practice breaches this regulation, account shall be taken of:

- timing, location, nature or persistence

- use of threatening or abusive language or behaviour

- exploitation by the trader of any specific misfortune or circumstance that impairs the consumer's judgement, in order to influence the consumer's decision with regard to the product

- any onerous or disproportionate non-contractual barrier imposed by the trader where a consumer wishes to exercise rights under the contract (for example, rights to terminate the contract or switch to another product or trader)

- any threat to take action that cannot legally be taken

Note: 'coercion' includes the use of physical force, and 'undue influence' means exploiting a position of power in relation to the consumer so as to apply pressure, even without the use of (or threatening to use) physical force, in a way that significantly limits the consumer's ability to make an informed decision.

4. General duty not to trade unfairly (regulation 3)

This is effectively failing to act in accordance with reasonable expectations of acceptable trading practice. Regulations 3(1) and 3(3) set out a general prohibition of unfair business to consumer practices and will allow action to be taken in relation to unfair practices which do not fit into the more specific prohibitions. This will cover a wide range of unfair practices including practices which may emerge in the future.

The general prohibition prohibits practices that:

- contravene the requirements of professional diligence (defined as the standard of special skill and care that a trader may reasonably be expected to exercise towards consumers which is commensurate with either honest market practice in the trader's field of activity, or the general principle of good faith in the trader's field of activity)

- materially distort the economic behaviour of the average consumer (or are likely to) with regard to the product (that is, appreciably to impair the average consumer's ability to make an informed decision thereby causing him to take a transactional decision that he would not have taken otherwise)

What are the consequences of non-compliance?

Enforcers may take civil enforcement action in respect of a breach of the CPRs under Part 8 of the Enterprise Act 2002. This can be done by applying to a court for an enforcement order and a breach of any order could lead to up to two years' imprisonment and/or an unlimited fine.

The CPRs also contain criminal offences that can be prosecuted by the Office of Fair Trading (OFT), trading standards services, or the Department of Enterprise, Trade & Investment in Northern Ireland (and by the Lord Advocate in Scotland). The penalties are:

- on summary conviction, a fine not exceeding the statutory maximum (currently £5,000)

- on conviction on indictment, an unlimited fine or imprisonment for up to two years (or both)

****

Chapter 11

Unsafe Goods

Sometimes the consumer purchases a good which, when tested, turns out to be unsafe. If a contract exists between the consumer and retailer then the Sale of Goods Act s14 will give protection. If no such contract exists then the Consumer Protection Act will apply.

The Consumer Protection Act 1987 also provides for criminal liability. The claim must be made within three years of the date the damage was caused, or three years from the date the damage could reasonably have been discovered. The manufacturers or importers liability ends ten years after the goods first appeared on the market.

The Consumer Protection Act is not aimed at shoddy goods, but at unsafe goods. The Act sets out a general offence of supplying consumer goods which are not reasonably safe, provides for safety regulations to be made for products and provides for a system of notices to assist trading standards officers to enforce the Act.

Many consumer goods are controlled, or the safety of goods is controlled by detailed regulations related to the manufacture of a particular good. However, the Consumer Protection Act provides for a general safety standard. Section 19 of the Act defines what is "safe" and states: 'Safe' in relation to any goods means that there is no risk, or no risk apart from one reduced to a minimum. Therefore, goods do not have to be 100% safe'. This is probably an impossibility. However, the risk of unsafe goods must be reduced to a minimum.

A person is guilty of an offence if he supplies any consumer goods which fail to comply with the general safety requirement, offers or agrees to supply any such good or exposes or possesses any such goods for supply.

Section 10 (1) and (2) are the relevant sections of the Act and section 10(2) contains a list of factors to be taken into account.

There are, as with all areas of law, recognised defences to the supply of unsafe goods. The important ones are:

a) the goods conform in a relevant respect with a European Community obligation;

b) the goods conform to any applicable safety regulations or safety standards set out by the Secretary of State for Trade and Industry for the purpose of the general safety requirement

c) that the offenders reasonably believed that the goods would not be used or consumed in the United Kingdom;

d) that the goods were supplied in the course of a business and that at the time the retailer did not know or had no reasonable grounds for believing that the goods failed to comply with the general safety requirements.;

e) that the goods were not supplied as new. The general safety requirement does not apply to second hand goods.

Penalties for contravention of the law can be up to £5,000 fine or six months in prison. However, this can vary greatly and a trader on trial for manslaughter can expect a higher sentence. In addition to the above, the General Product Safety Regulations 2005 give a consumer protection against the sale or manufacture of goods that are unsafe.

You do not have to have been injured by the goods for an offence to have been committed. Most new, second-hand and reconditioned goods are covered by these regulations unless there is a specific European safety law that applies.

The European Community has been very active in this area and the current position is that a General Product Safety Directive has been issued to standardise the safety of food throughout Europe and was introduced onto the Statute books in 1999. Also, the Toy Safety Regulations 1995, based on a European Directive, governs the safety of toys and will give specific information on what constitutes a safe toy.

If you feel any product is unsafe you should contact The Citizens Advice Consumer Service on 0845 404 0505. (This service replaced Consumer Direct in March 2012).

****

Chapter 12

Package Holidays

There are various common law protections in the case of holidays. However, the main area of consumer protection in the case of package holidays are the Package Travel, Package Holidays and Package Tours Regulations 1992 and the ABTA Code of practice.

The Regulations were introduced to comply with EU Directive 90/314 on Package Holidays and Package Tours. The directive was inevitable because of the level of tourism across EU member states. Most consumer problems related to holidays concern differences between the holiday description on booking and the actual reality. It is possible in these circumstances that there is also an offence under s14 Trade Descriptions Act 1978.

The Package Travel, Package Holidays and Package Tours Regulations 1992

The definition of 'package holidays'.
The Regulations do not alter the existing common-law protections but add significant duties on tour operators. The Regulations apply to all package holidays-but the word 'package' is given a very broad definition in Regulation 2 (1): the prearranged combination of at least two of the following components when sold or offered for sale at an inclusive price and when the service covers a period of more than 24 hours or includes overnight accommodation:
  a) transport
  b) accommodation

c)   other tourist services not ancillary to transport or accommodation and accounting for a significant proportion of the package and

i)   submission of separate accounts for different components shall not cause the arrangement to be other than a package

ii)   the fact that a combination is arranged at the request of the consumer in accordance with his specific instructions (whether modified or not) shall not of itself cause it to be treated as other than prearranged,

Information to be given by the holiday operator before the contract is concluded

The basic common law rules on formation can apply. The brochure is generally seen as an invitation to treat. But the Regulations, in Regulation 9, provide certain safeguards by ensuring that certain information is given to the consumer before the contract is concluded, and that the information is comprehensible to the consumer. The necessary information is detailed in schedule 2:

- the intended destination
- the intended means of travel
- the exact dates and the place of departure
- the locality of accommodation and its classification
- meals that are included in the package
- the minimum number of travellers to allow the holiday to go ahead
- any relevant itineraries, visits or excursions
- the names and full addresses of the organiser, retailer and insurer

- the price and any details with regard to revising the price
- the payment schedule and method of payment
- any other necessary details, such as specific arrangements for diet etc, that have been indicated by the consumer
- the method and period for complaints to be made.

This information must be given to the consumer both before the contract is made and in the contract itself. This will not apply to late bookings. Failure to comply is a breach under regulation 9(3) and the operator is then prevented from relying on terms that are not sufficiently explained in this way - and the consumer may also cancel the holiday.

Statements made in holiday brochures

The common law distinction between terms and `trade puffs' applies where no reasonable person could rely on the statement. But, in any case, by regulation 4, holiday operators will be liable if they supply misleading information in their descriptive matter.

Liability
Terms and performance of the contract

By regulation 15(1) the operator is liable for the improper performance of the contract by other service providers. The only exception is where the improper performance is neither the fault of the operator nor of any other service provider:

- including where it is the fault of the consumer
- or where it is caused by the unforeseeable and unavoidable act of the third party; and
- where forces majeure applies, e.g. hurricanes

The ABTA Code of Practice also requires that it should be a term of all contracts for package holidays that the operator will accept liability for the

81

acts or omissions of their employees, agents, sub-contractors and suppliers which results in death, injury or illness-and that the operators will offer advice, guidance and financial assistance of up to £5000 to consumers on holiday who suffer death, injury or illness.

Alterations to the holiday

Alteration depends on the terms of the contract-a common term allows alteration to the itinerary. If an alteration amounts to non-performance then it is a breach of the contract by the operator and will be classed as a breach of the condition allowing the consumer to repudiate and claim back the cost of the holiday.

The ABTA Code Clause 2.4 requires operators to offer suitable alternatives in the case of cancellation or alteration.

Overbooking of flights

Passengers who are denied travel because of overbooking are entitled to a choice/combination of:

- reimbursement of the cost of the ticket
- re-routing to the destination at the earliest moment
- re-routing at a later date, at the passengers convenience
- compensation

There are special rules applying to overbooked flights from airports in the European Union. The rules also apply to flights from airports outside the EU but flying into an EU airport, on an EU airline.

These rules apply only if you were not allowed to board the flight, not if you volunteered to take a different flight. You must have a valid ticket and have met check in deadlines at the airport. If these conditions are met then you will be entitled to a full refund of your ticket and a free return flight to your first point of departure, if needed, or another flight either as soon as possible or at a later date of your choice. You will also be entitled to:

- compensation. The amount you get will depend on the circumstances, i.e. how late you were as a result of the overbooking
- compensation for two telephone calls, e mails or other forms of communication
- reasonable meals and refreshments if you have to wait for a later flight
- Hotel accommodation if appropriate (stay overnight until next flight)

If the above EU rules don't apply then you should check the terms and conditions with the operator.

Remember, the law applies to this area as it does to all other areas and the operator cannot opt out. If you are not satisfied with what has happened then you should contact ABTA who run an arbitration scheme (address at the back of the book).

You can also contact the Association of Independent Tour Operators on www.abta.com.

Insolvency of the tour operator

The Package Travel, Package Holidays and package Tours Regulations 1992 apply. Under regulation 16(1) tour operators must at all times be able to satisfy evidence of sufficient funds to be able to return deposits in the event of insolvency. Consumers who pay by credit card are also protected under the Consumer Credit Act 1974.

ABTA bonding arrangements ensure that a consumer is not left stranded when a tour operator goes into insolvency during his/her holidays.

Remedies

Damages are usually awarded on the basis of difference in value between what was contracted for and what was provided. Incidental losses are also possible. Claims are also possible for physical discomfort. Operators are, basically, liable for all losses that arise from the breach.

Recent developments in the law

The Office of Fair Trading issued guidance to tour operators on March 2004. The OFT believes that many standard form terms in contracts fall short of the requirements of the Unfair Contract terms In Consumer Contract Regulations 1999 and has suggested alternative wording for operators to avoid liability.

These include:

- standard terms on responsibility for errors and changes in invoices or brochures,
- the acceptance of responsibility for statements made by agents, employees and representatives
- Right to transfer holidays when prevented from travelling
- Price revision clauses
- Rights on cancellation and alteration
- The right to compensation and the amount of compensation
- Cancellation by the consumer
- Cancellation charges for failure to pay deposit of balance
- Rights where services not supplied during the holiday
- Exclusion of liability
- Reporting of complaints
- 'Read and understand' declarations

****

Chapter 13

Food safety

In the previous chapter we looked at the rights of the consumer and unsafe goods. In this chapter we look at the all-important area of food and health and safety.

Food poisoning is an increasing problem in our society and in the last decade there has been a massive increase in the number of reported cases. The major protection for the consumer in this area is the 1990 Food Safety Act, as amended by the General Food Regulations 2004. In addition, the Food Safety Act Amendment Regulations 2004 brought the Act in line with EU Regulation EC/178/2002.

The aim of the 1990 Act is to control all aspects of food safety throughout the food distribution chain. Breaches of the Act result in criminal liability. There is an unlimited fine attached to breaches of the Act and also a maximum prison term of two years.

Section 7 of The 1990 Food Safety Act creates a specific offence of rendering food injurious to health with the intent that it should be sold for human consumption. The offence can be committed in several ways:

a) by adding any article or substance to the food
b) by using any article or substance as an ingredient in the preparation of food
c) abstracting any constituent from the food;
d) subjecting the food to any other process or treatment.
Section 8 of the Act also creates a number of offences and states:

"Any person who sells for human consumption or offers, exposes or advertises for sale for such consumption or has in his possession for the purpose of such sale or of preparation for such sale any food which fails to comply with food safety requirements shall be guilty of an offence"

Food can be unfit for human consumption even if it poses no health hazard. This is relevant to food which has started to incur mould growth.

The Food Safety Act also deals with food which misleads consumers. Section 14 states that anyone who sells food which is, by substance, not of the nature and quality demanded by the consumer is guilty of an offence, namely that of misleading the consumer. There are many examples here, particularly concerning meat and meat substitutes, i.e., fat instead of mince and fish. Section 15 of the Act Deals with the labelling of food and attempts to mislead by false claims. The Act also contains many powers for food inspectors to inspect and seize food and to close down premises. There are, as with the other areas of law, defences to breaches of the Act. One main defence is that of due diligence. However, in common with the other areas, defences have to be sound and backed up with concrete evidence.

The Food Standards Act 1999

The Act was introduced in the House of Commons on 10 June 1999 and received Royal Assent on 11 November 1999.

The main purpose of the Act is to establish the Food Standards Agency, provide it with functions and powers, and to transfer to it certain functions in relation to food safety and standards under other Acts. The Act gives effect to the proposals of the White Paper, 'The Food Standards Agency: A Force for Change' (Cm 3830).

It sets out the Agency's main objective of protecting public health in relation to food and the functions that it will assume in pursuit of that aim, and gives the Agency the powers necessary to enable it to act in the consumer's interest at any stage in the food production and supply chain.

The Act provides for the Agency's main organisational and accountability arrangements. In addition, it provides powers to establish a scheme for the notification of the results of tests for food-borne diseases.

****

Chapter 14
Consumer Remedies

There are a number of remedies available to the consumer. The Principal remedy is that through the civil courts-more specifically the small claims court, which is part of the county court. However, before using the small claims court, it may be necessary to consider other remedies, such as an Alternative Dispute Resolution scheme.

These schemes use a third party, such as an arbitrator or an ombudsman to help the consumer and supplier of goods or services to reach a solution. You will usually have to complete the suppliers internal complaints scheme beforehand and a fee may be payable to use the scheme. This is usually refunded if you are successful. Some schemes are legally binding, which means that you can't take court action if you aren't satisfied with the decision, except to enforce an award. If the claim is over £5,000 then the use of ADR should be discussed with a solicitor.

Advantages of ADR
The main advantages are:

- you may resolve your problem
- you may be awarded compensation
- the procedure is less formal than going to court
- in some schemes the decision may be binding on the trader but not on you, leaving you free to pursue further action through the courts
- it may cost less than going to court
- the procedure is confidential

Some potential disadvantages or points to think about

- the costs involved. Do a cost comparison before committing to ADR
- would you prefer to have a hearing so that your point can be put across in person
- if the arbitrators decision is legally binding, it will prevent you taking the matter through the courts
- you may have to pay further costs to enforce the arbitrators decision through the courts

Types of ADR

The main types of ADR that deal with consumer disputes are conciliation, arbitration or mediation. They are usually provided by trade associations, if you wish to use one of these schemes you should ask the supplier whether they are members of a trade association and if they are contact the association to find out whether they offer ADR.

Conciliation

In consumer disputes conciliation is the first stage in the arbitration process. The conciliator is usually a member of the trade association. Both the consumer and supplier will be asked to give written details of the complaint, including evidence and the conciliator will give an opinion on the best solution. Decisions are not binding leaving the way free for court action or arbitration.

Arbitration

Arbitration is a procedure for settling disputes in which both the consumer and the supplier usually agree to accept the decision of the arbitrator as legally binding. This means that court action cannot be taken except to enforce the award if the supplier doesn't pay.

The arbitrator will make a decision based on written evidence provided by the supplier and consumer. The decision is confidential.

Some contracts for services include an arbitration clause stating that you will refer any dispute to arbitration. Although this is binding once you have signed the agreement, if the total cost is below the small claims limit (£5,000) you cannot be forced to arbitrate unless you gave your agreement after the dispute arose.

Mediation

If a mediation scheme is used, the mediator will help consumer and supplier to negotiate an acceptable agreement and will act as a go between if you don't want to meet. If the supplier agrees to mediation, then both sides will be asked to give details of the dispute, including supplying evidence and will be asked to sign a mediation agreement. This will give the framework for mediation. If an agreement is reached then both sides will be asked to sign a draft terms of settlement. This will be legally binding unless it is stated otherwise. Mediation can be expensive but the Community Legal Service may provide help under the legal help scheme or the public funded legal representation scheme, depending on your circumstances.

Ombudsman schemes

Many services have an Ombudsman scheme that can be used by the consumer. Many financial services, for example, are covered by an Ombudsman scheme. You will only be able to refer the matter to the Ombudsman after you have exhausted the supplier's internal complaints scheme. The Ombudsman will make a recommendation or ruling, usually accepted by the supplier but which is not legally binding. However, a court will take an Ombudsman's ruling into account when making a decision. All Ombudsman's schemes are free.

Locating an ADR scheme

If you wish to pursue ADR then the first action is to find out whether the trader is a member of a trade association that offers such a service. If you experience any difficulty then you should contact Citizens Advice on 08454 04 05 05. The Law Society also has a Civil and Commercial Mediation Panel to help members of the public find qualified solicitor mediators. To obtain more details about this panel phone 0207 242 1222.

For further help you should contact the Chartered Institute of Arbitrators, 12 Bloomsbury Square, London WC1A 2LP Tel 020 7421 7444.

If, for whatever reason it is not possible to resolve the dispute through ADR, then it may be necessary to pursue the case through the small claims court.

What follows is a description of the small claims procedure and of remedies available to the aggrieved consumer. Following this there will be a description of other remedies, such as the office of fair-trading.

The Small Claims Court

The first fact to be aware of when taking a trader to court in order to obtain some sort of compensation is that it is not necessary to have either legal knowledge or use a solicitor when using the small claims procedure in the County Court.

Commencing a claim

A person can start legal action in any court and if the case is defended the court will decide what procedure to use. If the case is a simple one, with a value of £5000 or less, the court will decide that the small claims procedure will be used and will allocate the case to the small claims track. In most cases, the court will not order that costs are paid by the losing party in a small claims case. For this reason, most people do not use a solicitor when making a small claim. It may, however, be possible to get legal help using the legal help scheme.

Types of case dealt with in the small claims track

When the court is considering whether to allocate the case to a small claims track it will take into account a number of factors, but the main factor is the value of the case.

If the value of a case is £5000 or less it will generally be allocated to the small claims track. However, if it is a personal injury claim, it will be allocated to the small claims track only if the value of the claim for the personal injuries is not more than £1000. If the claimant is a tenant and is claiming against their landlord because repairs are needed to the premises and the cost of the work is £1000 or less, the case will be allocated to the small claims track.

Types of claims in the small claims court

The most common types of small claims are:

- Compensation for faulty goods, for example washing machines or other goods that go wrong
- Compensation for faulty services provided, for example by builders, garages and so on
- Disputes between landlords and tenants, for examples, rent arrears, compensation for not doing repairs
- Wages owed or money in lieu of notice

If a case proves to be too complex then a judge may refer the case to another track for a full hearing, even if below the limit for that track.

Actions before applying to court

Before applying to court it is always necessary to try to solve the problem amicably, or as amicably as possible without recourse to legal action. We have already discussed ADR. A person who intends to commence a claim should write a 'letter before action' which should set out terms for settlement before applying to court.

For example, if a television is defective, or workmanship on a car is faulty, there is no point applying to court for compensation before contacting the garage or repair shop. Whilst this may seem obvious, there are cases where people do rush in. Always try to settle before launching court action. It will assist in the case if it does go to court.

Which court deals with a small claim

The court action can be started in any court, but the case can be transferred. If the claim is defended and the claim is for a fixed amount, the court will automatically transfer the case to a defendant's local court (if he or she is an individual not a company). In other cases, either party can ask for the case to be transferred.

Commencing a claim

The claimant commences a claim by filling in a claim form, obtainable from local county courts or legal stationers. They can also be obtained from the internet. The government court site is www.justice.gov.uk. All forms can be obtained from this website as can a host of information on all legal topics.

The form is quite straightforward and asks for details of claimant and defendant and how much is owed. The form also asks for the particulars of the claim. The particulars set out full details of the claim. If there is not enough room on the form then a separate piece of paper can be used. The claimant has a right to spend a little more time on the particulars and can send them to the defendant separately, but no later than 14 days after the claim form.

The forms are designed to be user friendly and are accompanied by guidance notes to ensure that no mistakes are made.

The claimant may be entitled to claim interest on the claim and, if so, must give details of the interest claimed in the particulars of claim. In a personal injury claim the particulars of claim must include the claimant's date of birth and brief details of the injuries. The claimant must attach a list of any past expenses and losses that they want to claim for and any expenses and losses that they may incur in the future.

Applying for the claim form to be issued

The claimant must ensure that two copies of the claim form reach the court where court action is to commence and a copy should be kept for records. There will be a fee to pay. Currently this depends on the amount of money to be claimed. You should check with your local county court, small claims division, for the current fees.

In some cases, the fee will be waived, for example if the claimant is receiving income support, working families tax credit, disabled persons tax credit or income based job seekers allowance. If none of these benefits are received, but financial hardship would be suffered if a fee was paid, the fee may also be waived. The court will stamp the claim form and then, in most cases, serve it on the defendant. The court will give the claimant a notice of issue.

Usually the court will serve the claim form by sending it to the defendant by first class post. The claimant will be deemed to have received it on the second day of posting. If the claimant wishes to serve the claim form his or herself then a request should be made and the court will provide the form and other forms that go with it.

If the case is not defended

If the defendant is not defending the case, then he or she may accept that they owe the money. If this is the case then he or she can pay the money directly to the claimant. If the defendant has accepted that they owe the money, but needs time to pay, they can propose an arrangement, for example that the amount owed is paid in instalments or all the money in one lump sum on a specified future date. If the claimant accepts this offer, he or she will have to return a form to the court requesting 'judgement by admission'. If the defendant does not keep to this agreement the claimant can then take enforcement action.

If the claimant does not accept this offer then he or she must give good reason and a court official will decide what a reasonable arrangement will be. The court will send both parties an order for payment. If the claimant is not happy with the order then he or she will have to write to the court giving reasons and sending a copy to the defendant. A judge will then decide what is reasonable for the defendant to pay. If the defendant does not keep to the arrangement, the claimant can take enforcement action.

If the defendant is defending the case

If the case is to be defended, the defendant has to respond to the claim within 14 days of service (this is the second day of posting). If the particulars of claim were served after the claim form the defendant must respond within 14 days of service of particulars of claim. A defence is launched by the defendant sending back the defence form, which was sent with the claim form.

If the defendant does not send a defence back within the time period then the claimant can ask for an order to be made against him or her. The defendant can send the defence back to the court or can send the acknowledgement of service form sent with the defence form back to court and the defence form back within 14 days of this. This helps if more time is needed. When the defence is sent to the court the court will send an allocation questionnaire to both the claimant and the defendant. This must be returned to the court no later than the date specified in it. When the claimant returns the allocation form a fee should also be sent although this can be waived on financial grounds. The court will use the information contained within the allocation questionnaire to decide which track to allocate the case to.

When the court has decided to allocate the case to the small claims track, the claimant and defendant will be sent a notice of allocation. This form will tell the parties what they have to do to prepare for the hearing. These instructions are called 'directions'. One example of directions may be that parties are told that they should send all copies of relevant documents to court, documents that they intend to use in court in the case against the other party. These are sent at least 14 days before the case begins.

There are standard directions for a number of common cases, for example, if the claim is to do with a holiday then there will be standard directions from the courts as to the evidence needed.

The day of the hearing

The notice of allocation will usually specify the time, day and date of hearing, where the hearing will take place and how much time has been allowed for it. If the claimant wants to attend the hearing but for some reason cannot, then a letter should be sent to the court requesting a different hearing date. A fee is payable and the court will only agree to this request if it is based on reasonable grounds.

A claimant can also ask the court to deal with a claim in his or her absence. A typical case might be where the costs and time to reach the court are disproportionate. If this is the case then a letter should reach the court at least seven days before the case.

In some cases, the court will not set a final hearing date. The following are alternatives used by the courts:

- The court could propose that the case is dealt with without a hearing. If both parties have no objections then the case can be decided on the papers only. If the parties do not reply by the date given then the court will usually take that silence as consent
- The court may hold a preliminary hearing. This could happen if the claim requires special directions which the judge wants to explain to the parties personally or where the judge feels that the claimant or defendant has no real prospect of succeeding and wants to sort out the claim as soon as possible to save everyone time and expense, or if the papers do not show any reasonable grounds for bringing the claim. A preliminary hearing could become a final hearing where the case is decided.

Preparing a case

It is important that a case is prepared carefully – the court has to be convinced. A reasonable amount of time should be spent ensuring that all the facts are entered, all dates specified and all paperwork is available.

The following points are a general guide to what preparation should be made:

- someone with low income can use the legal help scheme to cover the costs of legal advice, but not representation from a solicitor. This advice can be extremely useful and can include getting expert reports, for example on faulty goods. However, a report can only be used in court with permission of the court
- notes about the case should be set out in date order. This will help you to present your case and will make sense to a judge. All backing documentation should be taken to court and be presented

if asked for. This documentation should be organised around the presentation, in chronological order

- damaged or faulty goods should be taken as evidence. If it is not possible to do this then photographs should be taken instead
- evidence of expenses should be taken along and any receipts kept
- all letters about the case should be taken to court
- in most cases, the claimant and defendant may be the only witnesses. If the court has agreed that other witnesses can attend, then they must attend. If a witness has difficulty getting time off work then a witness summons can be served. The courts will explain how to do this.

The final hearing

The final hearing is usually held in public but can be held in private if the parties agree or the judge thinks that it is necessary. Hearings in the small claims track are informal and the usual rules of evidence do not apply. The judge can adopt any method of dealing with the hearing that he or she thinks fit and can also ask questions of the witnesses before anyone else. A lay representative has the right to speak on behalf of a person at a hearing but only if that party attends the hearing. If an interpreter is needed, because English is not the first language then an experienced advisor should be consulted, or the court may be able to advise on this.

At the end of the hearing the judge will pass judgement. The judge has to give reasons for the decision that he or she has arrived at. If the claimant wins, he or she will get the court fee back as well as the sum awarded. If the claimant loses no fees will be returned. However, it is unlikely that any other costs will have to be paid.

Appealing against a decision

A party may appeal against a judgement in the small claims track only if the court made a mistake in law or there was a serious irregularity in the proceedings. If a person wishes to appeal then a notice of appeal must be filed within 14 days. A fee is payable although this can be waived in cases of financial hardship. If you do wish to appeal a decision, it is very likely that you would need to consult a solicitor or an experienced advisor to help you.

Enforcement of orders

If a defendant does not pay, the claimant can go back to court and enforce that order. As we have seen, there are a number of remedies, such as bailiff, attachment of earnings and garnishee order. Another fee is involved when enforcing. The court will give you full details of different remedies and fees involved.

****

Chapter 15

Consumer Issues Generally

Buying goods in the European Union

When buying goods or purchasing services in a member country of the European Union (The EU) your rights will be based on the law existing in that particular country. The fact that EU law is continuously pushing for harmonisation means that rights will be similar in member countries. You will have UK statutory rights and also the rights of the country where the goods were purchased if:

- you signed a contract for goods or services with a seller based in another EU country but the seller advertised in the UK and you concluded the contract in the UK. One example is you purchased clothes mail order from a company based in Spain, having seen the advert in a UK magazine and ordered from the UK;

- the seller received your order while in the UK; or

- you bought the goods and services in another UE member state during an excursion organised by the seller to encourage you to buy goods or services.

You will not usually be entitled to UK statutory rights as well as those of the country of purchase if the contract involves:

- a service is provided which is not usually provided in the UK

- transport-there are some exceptions to this, including package travel contracts

- Insurance

- Land or property-although timeshare has its own specific rules (see below)

If you buy something from the internet and the seller is based in another EU member state then in most cases you will have the same statutory rights as if you had bought it from a seller based in the UK. There is a voluntary membership scheme for traders throughout the UK who use websites to sell goods or services. This is called the Euro-label scheme and members must comply with a code of conduct. There is more information about this scheme on www.euro-label.com.

In the main, you will not have to pay more VAT or tax when you buy goods or services in another EU country. However, special rules apply in relation to certain goods such as nearly new cars, motorbikes and boats. More advice can be obtained from HM Revenue and Customs about these goods.

Faulty goods

The law in each EU country will determine whether or not you can return faulty goods or right faulty services, repair them or get your money back. Guarantees too will be affected by the law in the country of purchase.

If a problem arises

The response to discovering that a good or service is faulty is the same as that in England: stop using the goods; find proof of purchase; if the goods in question are dangerous phone Citizens Advice Consumer Line on 0845 404 0505; contact the seller.

You could write to the seller, alternatively you could use the European Consumer Complaint Form. You can obtain a copy of this from the internet by going to the address: Asserting Consumer Rights Section at http://europa.eu/geninfo and then searching for the consumer complaint form.

If you are not satisfied with the response from the supplier then you should determine whether or not the company/person is a member of an organisation that offers conciliation or mediation. If you paid for the goods on credit, e.g. a credit card, then it may be simpler to make a claim against the credit company rather than the seller. The goods would usually have cost over £100 and under £30,000. If you are going nowhere with your complaint, and feel that there was a problem with the advertising, then you can try the Advertising Standards Authority, which is a member of the European Standards Alliance. Refer to useful addresses at the back of the book.

European Consumer Centres

There is a network of European Consumer Centres (ECC's) in many of the EU countries which provide information about consumer law and the procedures for enforcing your rights. Visit https://ec.europa.eu/consumers/index/en_htm

Timeshare property

As most people know who have been pursued through the streets by agents, buying a timeshare buys you the right to use holiday accommodation for a set amount of time each year, i.e. one week or two weeks at a select resort or resorts. To be protected by timeshare laws, the agreement must be for at least three years. What is described below relates to timeshares purchased from companies and not private individuals.

When you buy a timeshare, it is important to remember that you are signing a binding agreement with a timeshare company. It is difficult to cancel the agreement so it is important to get as much information before you sign, including:

- full costs, including all charges

- length of agreement-if you are signing a contract for less than three years this is usually a deliberate attempt to avoid the law

- what the area and particular resort is like

- what you legal interest is in the property and terms and conditions of the agreement

- whether there is an owners committee or association and the extent of their powers

Complaining if things go wrong

A criminal offence may have been committed if you buy a timeshare in an EEA country (see below) and:

- you ask for a brochure and this is not provided; or

- the seller takes money off you during the cooling off period (see below); or

- the seller makes false or misleading claims about the timeshare.

If you have a problem and the above applies the contact Citizens Advice Consumer line on 0845 404 0505.

Cancelling a timeshare agreement

As with other consumer transaction, once you have signed a timeshare agreement, the law gives you a cooling off period during which time you can cancel the agreement and have your money back without having to pay a cancellation fee. You are entitled to a cooling off period only if the timeshare agreement is more than three years and is for a property or caravan in the EU area. This does not apply to timeshares bought before 1ˢᵗ May 2004 in countries which joined the EU before this date, i.e. Malta.

The length of the cooling off period depends on the country that you were in when the agreement was signed. If you signed the agreement in the UK the cooling off period is 14 days. In a Member Country of the European Economic Area (EEA) the cooling off period is ten days. In some EEA countries it will be necessary for a lawyer to witness the agreement. This is non-refundable if you cancel the agreement. In general, the EEA consists of EU Member states, although this should be checked with the EU website.

Timeshare companies in the UK and EEA must tell you about the cooling off period when you sign the agreement. If they don't then it will usually be extended by three months.

If there are problems with your timeshare, and thankfully over the last decade a lot of the rogues have disappeared, then your rights will very much depend on what agreement you have signed. You may need the help of a specialist lawyer to decide what law applies and the Organisation for Timeshare in Europe www.timeshare.org.uk/otecode will be able to assist in finding one.

The Timeshare Consumers Association can also provide help and assistance. They can be contacted on 01909 591100 or www.timeshare.org.uk .

Payment protection insurance (PPI)

Everyone has witnessed the trouble that banks have experienced as a result of miss selling of PPI. Huge amounts of compensation have been paid out. It is very important to understand what PPI is, do you want it and the benefits and when to buy.

Payment protection insurance (PPI) covers loan or debt repayments if you are unable to meet them in certain situations, such as being made redundant or not being able to work because of an accident or illness.

You may have been offered or sold a PPI policy at the same time as you took out a loan, mortgage, credit card, store card, car finance or other credit. However, from 6 April 2012 a firm generally can not sell PPI at the same time as you take out credit.

You do not have to buy PPI from the same firm and it usually pays to shop around for a deal that is right for you.

This type of cover may also be called loan protection, credit insurance, loan repayment insurance, ASU (accident, sickness and unemployment) insurance, account cover or payment cover.

How PPI covers you

The benefits of PPI and how the policy works vary depending on the terms and conditions. It will generally cover monthly loan or mortgage repayments, or at least some of them, for a set period of time. This will usually be for up to 12 months but some policies can cover your repayments for a longer period.

With credit and store cards, PPI may pay a percentage of your outstanding balance or the minimum payment each month for up to a year. This might only be for the amount you owe when you make a claim, and not any balance you build up after this.

Once the claim period has ended you will have to make any outstanding repayments yourself.

If the policy includes life insurance it will generally pay off the balance of the loan or debt if you die.

Before you buy PPI

As PPI policies can differ greatly you should shop around to find one that includes the features you need.

You should always read the key policy information before you buy. This sets out information like how long the cover lasts, the main features and benefits of the policy, and any significant or unusual exclusions or conditions.

Some PPI policy features to consider include:

- the price of the policy;
- whether you have other insurance which could cover your repayments;
- any limits on the amount of benefit you may receive from a claim on the policy;
- the period of time the policy will cover your loan or debt repayments;
- whether the cover starts as soon as you make a claim or after a certain amount of time;
- the types of injuries and accidents covered, and those that may be excluded (e.g. stress or back complaints);
- whether it covers injuries or illness that you have had before taking out the policy;
- how long you have to be employed on a permanent contract before you can make a claim; and
- whether the policy covers you if you are self-employed.

PPI is not the only product that can protect you against loss of income and may not always be the right one for your circumstances. A couple of alternatives are income protection, which is not linked to a debt but covers loss of income, and short-term protection insurance.

Travel Insurance

Many of us have had problems abroad and have claimed, or tried to claim, on our travel insurance. Travel insurance can provide you with cover for cancelling or cutting short a trip for specific reasons outside of your control, i.e. illness, missed transport or delayed departure for reasons outside your control, medical and other emergency expenses, personal injury or death and lost, stolen or damaged property.

Travel insurance can be purchased for a single or multiple journey and should be taken out prior to any trip. You should check your household contents policy as this may cover certain elements such as damaged or stolen property when abroad. Your credit card company may also provide an element of cover. This should be checked.

When you take out a policy it is important to tell the insurer about anything which may affect the claim, such as a pre-existing condition for which you may need to get treatment whilst you are away. Withholding information can affect the insurer's decision to pay out on any future claim.

Making a claim

If you need to claim on a travel insurance policy:

- check that you are within the time limits for making a claim

- check that you are covered for the situation you are claiming for and what the maximum amount is

- check the policy for any terms and conditions that need to be met

- contact your insurer as soon as possible to inform them of the intended claim and to request a claim form. Always keep copies of forms.

Make a report to police within 24 hours of the incident. This is very important. If you cannot do this then make a report as soon as possible. Keep all receipts for replacements etc. If you need medical treatment contact the insurer to get authorisation for this.

In some European countries, you can get free urgent medical treatment if you have form EHIC. In addition, many more countries have health care agreements with the UK which mean that you might be able to get free emergency treatment. For more information freephone 00800 67891011 or go to www.nhs.uk/nhsengland/Healthcareabroad

Travel insurance will cover you if you are pregnant as long as you are in good health.

Cancelling or shortening your trip

Your insurer will only meet a claim for the above if good reason for shortening or cancelling can be shown. This can include:

- unexpected illness, injury or death of you, a partner or travel companion
- if a pregnant woman is advised not to travel for a medical reason which occurred after you took out the policy
- if you are called for jury service or a witness in court
- if a fire or some other unexpected damage occurs in your home
- if you are made redundant.

Complaints

If you feel that you have a complaint against a particular insurer then you should contact the Financial Services Authority, address at the back of this book. You can find out more also by visiting the website of the Financial Ombudsman www.financial-ombudsman.org.uk or phone them on 0800 023 4567.

If the insurance was purchased from a travel agent or tour operator then the situation is slightly different if your complaint is the way you were sold the policy. In this case, you will probably need to go to the small claims court.

Supplier of goods/services has gone out of business

If the supplier has gone out of business your action and the outcome will very much depend on the status of the trader, whether limited company, sole trader or partnership. If payments were made by credit card the credit card company may be liable if the amount is more than £100 and less than £30,000. This will not apply if the payment was made by debit card.

Sole trader/partnership

Sole traders or partnerships remain liable even if they have ceased to trade. You should get advice from Citizens Advice Consumer line before taking court action. It is only worth taking action if the trader is able to pay. If the trader has gone bankrupt then it is not worth pursuing the matter. You would need to join the queue of other creditors following notification of bankruptcy.

Limited company

If the supplier is a limited company, it may have gone into administration or liquidation. If the company goes into administration, an administrator will be appointed. The administrator will see if the company can be rescued or sold rather than being liquidated.

A limited company can go into voluntary liquidation following a shareholders decision that the company is no longer solvent. The company can also go into liquidation following a court order. Once in liquidation, a liquidator is appointed to redistribute all the company's assets. This is known as winding up. The liquidator will send the final accounts to the

Registrar of Companies and the company will be dissolved three months later.

You may be able to find out the status of a company by contacting Companies House on 0303 1234 500 or the website at www.companieshouse.co.uk

For all other matters in relation to money/goods/services owed then you should contact the liquidator of the company.

Dry cleaning

Dry cleaning is an area where significant numbers of people experience problems. As with other goods/services supplied, the law underpinning this particular service states that the dry cleaning must be carried out with care, finished within a reasonable time and provided at a reasonable cost to the consumer.

On the whole, dry cleaning can only achieve a finish that is dependant on the condition of the garment in the first place. It may serve to highlight existing wear and tear of the garment that cannot be claimed for. However, if you feel that the item has been poorly cleaned then it is reasonable to ask for a refund. You should allow the company to re-clean the product of offered.

Compensation may be payable if the contract was breached and the dry cleaning was not carried out in time or with care. It may also be payable if there has been negligence or any second cleaning has not solved the problem.

If you have a problem with dry cleaning you should take the item back and ask to speak to the manager or you should write a clear letter outlining the fault. Explain the problem and ask for refund, repair or compensation. Like many organisations, dry cleaning has its own umbrella organisation, the Textile Services Association (TSA). They provide a conciliation services if the dry cleaner in question is a member. They can be reached on 020 7843 9490. If they are not a member or you do not wish to use their services, you can obtain the services of an expert witness, such as an independent test house.   One such test house is the Dry Cleaning Technology Centre 01943 816545. At the end of the whole process, if the dry cleaner refuses to cooperate and you feel that you are getting nowhere then you can resort to the small claims court to solve your action. This will only be really feasible if you have tried all other avenues and you have kept all records and receipts along with the evidence.

Mobile phones

Many people experience problems with mobile phones and seek redress against the supplier. The phone, at the end of the day, is like other goods and services. The law says that it should:

- match its description
- be of satisfactory quality

These rights exist wherever you buy the phone (with the exception of purchase off a private individual.

You will not be successful in any action against a seller if you examined the phone and the fault was obvious but you went ahead and purchased the phone. Once bought, you cannot take action if you change your mind. Likewise, the usual stipulations exist concerning wear and tear.

The service from the mobile phone provider must be carried out with reasonable care and carried out in a reasonable time and delivered at a reasonable cost. The rules concerning credit cards or credit agreements apply to mobile phones as to all other goods.

If you have a problem with a handset it is the seller and not the manufacturer or service provider who is liable for rectifying the problem. If you have a problem with service then it is to the service provider that you should turn to seek redress.

If you bought the phone after 31st March 2003, you can ask the seller to repair or replace it free of charge if it is faulty. If you do this within six months of receiving the phone it will be assumed that the problem existed when you purchased it, unless the seller can demonstrate otherwise. You can still ask for a replacement or repair within six years of purchasing the phone if it is reasonable for it to have lasted that long. If it is impossible to replace or repair the phone and the fault persists then it is reasonable to ask for a full or partial refund. You may be entitled to some form of compensation if the phone is not fit for purpose, the contract with the provider has been breached, the phone is unsafe or dangerous, the seller has made a false statement or any repair undertaken or inadequate service has not rectified the problem.

There are several organisations that deal with complains against mobile phone companies. Office of the Telecommunications Ombudsman (OTELO) is chief amongst these. They can be contacted on 0330 440 1614 www. ombudsmanservices.org The Communication and Internet Services Adjudication Scheme (CISAS) may also be able to help. In common with many organisations that offer help, they will insist that you have exhausted the company's own complaints procedure first. They can be contacted on 020 7520 3814 or www.cisas.org.uk.

Private sales including boot sales

When goods are purchased from a private individual, either from an advert in the paper or from a boot sale, the law lays down the basic requirement that the goods must match their description, i.e. they must be as described by the seller. It is very important to check goods when you purchase them as the private seller is not liable for faulty goods. However, it is an offence for a private seller to sell a car that is un-roadworthy. If a business sells goods purporting to be a private seller then this is a criminal offence and you should contact Citizens Advice Consumer Line on 0845 4040 0505 immediately.

As with all other areas involving transactions between buyer and seller evidence of purchase should be kept along with all other evidence. This will be needed, as the final resort is the small claims court.

Remember, it is purchases of goods or services from a private vendor which offers the least legal protection.

Buying at auction

As with most other circumstances, when goods are purchased, they must match their description and be of satisfactory quality and fit for purpose. These requirements are set out in the Sale of Goods Act 1979. Your rights under this Act apply to all new goods bought at auction and also second hand goods purchased where you did not have the opportunity to attend to inspect the goods, i.e. internet auctions. If you buy at auction you may not have these rights if:

- the goods are second hand and you have the opportunity to attend the sale in person

- you are informed that the Sale of Goods Act 1979 does not apply or that goods are sold as seen and the auctioneer can demonstrate that this is reasonable.

When you purchase goods at auction you will enter into a contract with the owner of the goods, not the auctioneer. If there is a problem with the goods then you should take action against the owner of the goods not the auctioneer. The auction house is not under any obligation to give you the owner's details.

If you bought new goods at an auction after 31st March 2003, or second hand goods at an auction where you cannot attend in person you can ask the trader to replace the goods free of charge or repair them if faulty.

A last resort is the small claims court. However, remember that buying goods at auction can be similar to buying from a private individual and it is only worth pursuing a case if you feel confident of winning.

Remember, auctions, especially internet auctions are not the safest environments from which to purchase goods and the utmost care must be taken to ensure that money is not lost or goods are not faulty.

Banks and building societies

Banks are the same as other service providers when it comes to the provision of goods and services, they must carry out their business with reasonable care and skill, in reasonable time and at reasonable cost. This last point has been a bone of contention recently, particularly in relation to bank charges.

The Banking Code

The Banking Code sets out minimum standards of service for banks, building societies and credit card companies providing personal banking services. Although not mandatory to sign up to the code, most banks and building societies along with credit card companies do.

Banks and others signed up to the code must act fairly and in a reasonable manner in all its dealings with customers. If it breaches the code then in keeping with all other Ombudsman Services, you should first exhaust the complaints procedure of the bank or other concerned. After this has failed to rectify the matter then you can complain to the Financial Services Ombudsman (see below).

Bank charges

This is one area which has hit the headlines recently. Banks charging very high fees for unauthorised overdrawn customers. Banks and building societies are allowed to charge for their services, which must be clearly set out. Banks can charge default charges, being charges for typically exceeding your overdraft limit. The bank or building society is only allowed to charge what it costs to cover their administrative charges. This has not been the case, and if they charge you more than this you may have a legal right to be refunded the difference. If you think that your default charges are unreasonably high you should ask the bank to refund the difference. More information concerning this procedure can be found at www.which.net/campaigns.

If you approach a bank or building society with a complaint make sure that you have copies of all evidence (statements etc). Either speak to your account manager or write to the branch manager. If you are not satisfied with the response then you should ask for details of the complaints procedure. Find out whether the bank subscribes to the Banking Code of Practice. A copy of this code can be obtained either from the bank in question or from the British Bankers Association at www.bba.org.uk

When you have completed each stage of the internal complaints procedure of the organisation concerned you will be sent a letter of deadlock if the complaint has not been solved.

You can then use the Financial Ombudsman Service. Your complaint must be brought to the Ombudsman within six months of the deadlock letter. The Ombudsman will try to deal with your complaint informally but if this fails will make a preliminary decision. After the consumer and bank involved have made comments on this preliminary decision then the Ombudsman will make a final ruling or recommendation. If you are still not satisfied then you can take court action. the Ombudsman can be contacted on 0800 453 4567 or www.financial-ombudsman.org.uk.

Motor Insurance

If you drive a car or leave it parked on a road, then it must be insured. There are three main types of insurance:

- Third party which is the minimum amount of cover you can have. This covers you for damage to someone else's vehicle or property or injury to someone which arises as a result of an accident involving your car
- Third party fire and theft. This includes the above with the addition of theft and fire
- Comprehensive insurance. This includes the above two categories but also pays for repairs to your car and can cover you for a host of other eventualities if requested and paid for such as legal and medical, hire of another vehicle etc.

When taking out insurance it is necessary to give the insurer as much information as possible otherwise the policy could be invalidated. When you first take out insurance you will get a cover note. It is a criminal offence to drive without this cover note or a full policy note.

There may be certain circumstances where your insurance policy is found to be invalid. These can be:

- someone who is not on your policy drives your car
- your car is found to be unroadworthy-third party claims should still be accepted
- you do not have a valid driving licence
- the insurer believes that you are partly to blame for the accident-they may only pay part of the damage
- your insurer has gone out of business and cannot meet the claim. In this case you may be able to get compensation from the Financial Services Compensation Scheme (FCS). They can be

contacted on 020 7166 1000. If the insurer is a member of Lloyds contact the Lloyds Complaints Department on 020 7327 5693.

Stolen vehicle

If your car has been stolen you should inform the police and insurer immediately. The insurer will wait several weeks before settling the claim in case the car is found. If you were paying your premium by instalments you will usually need to pay the full year even if the car has been stolen. If the car is not found the insurer will usually pay the then current market value of the car, which is almost certain to be different than the price you paid for it.

Claiming if in an accident

If you have an accident you should never admit liability. This is a matter for the insurers and the police. Always exchange names and addresses and insurance details with the other driver(s). Always take the registration number. If, as sometimes happens, the other person refuses to give you details of their insurance your insurer may be able to trace the insurer via the registration number. Tell the insurer about the accident immediately. If someone has been injured or the other person is under the influence of drink or drugs call the police immediately.

If you are making a claim against the other driver write to them informing them of this. State that you hold them responsible for the accident and also send a copy of the letter to your insurer. The other driver must report the accident to their insurer before the matter can be dealt with. The insurer can only act on the instructions of their own policy holder. If you need to find out details of the other persons policy, or whether they have one you should look up the motor insurance database by contacting the Motor Insurers Bureau on www.mib.urg.uk

If the driver was uninsured or cannot be identified then the Motor Insurers Bureau may be able to settle your claim, even where the other driver is uninsured.

If you have a comprehensive policy then you should claim from your own insurer. You will still need to claim from the other drivers policy for any injuries suffered as a result of the accident or any losses which are not covered directly by your own policy.

One more important point to note. When claiming, always weigh the economic benefits up against the loss of your no-claims bonus.

Driving overseas

Your policy will cover you for third party to drive in a European Union Country if your insurer is EU based. Your policy may also include third party cover to drive in a non-EU country. You should check these details with your insurer. Your insurer can issue you with a green card to show that you have increased cover. It may be necessary in certain non-EU countries to show this.

Motor cycle insurance

There are two types of insurance covering motor cycles:

- Specified cycle policy which covers you to ride a specific motor cycle
- Rider policy which will cover you to ride any motorcycle up to a specified cc with the owner's permission.

Motor cycle insurance is usually limited to one person only. If someone else wants to ride your motor bike then they must be named on your policy or have their own policy. Generally, no-claims bonuses are not available for motorcycles.

If problems arise with your car or motor cycle insurance then it will, in common with other areas of goods and services, be necessary to exhaust your insurer's complaints procedure first. All insurers must be covered by the rules of the Financial Services Authority. This will mean that if you have a complaint, and you cannot resolve it with your insurer, and it is a legitimate complaint then you can take it to the Financial Ombudsman Service. For more information you should telephone 0800 023 4567 or go to their website on www.financial-ombudsman.org.uk

.

Dealing with Builders

This is an area that represents major problems for many people. Like many other providers of goods and services, when building work is carried out then it must be carried out with reasonable care and skill, finished within a reasonable time and provided at a reasonable cost. Goods or material provided must match their description and be of satisfactory quality.

However, before you can deal effectively with a building related problem you must first have a clear understanding of who your contract is with. It could be the builder, the architect/structural engineer (depending on the type and complexity of the work), the individual contractor or the subcontractor. Once identified then action can be taken. If you cannot identify who exactly is responsible then you should join them all in the action. You should also look into any guarantees that have been offered to see if they are relevant. Reliance on a guarantee does not take away your statutory right. As with other goods and services, special rules apply if you have used a credit card to pay. If the amount spent is over £100 or under £30,000 then the credit card company may be equally liable for any breach of contract.

Cancellation of building work

If you have recently signed a credit agreement away from the traders premises (i.e. at your own home) and the contract was signed after a face to face discussion with the trader, you may have a short period within which you can cancel (cooling off period). If the contract was signed on the traders business premises you may be able to withdraw from the agreement if you notify the credit company immediately and confirm the withdrawal in a letter sent by recorded delivery.

If you are not buying by credit but have signed a contract in your own home and wish to cancel, you should check the contract for cancellation rights. See above for advice about buying on the doorstep.

Finally, do not sign any documents or pay the final instalment due until you are totally satisfied. The majority of builders are honest and trustworthy. As with all walks of life there are the inadequate companies or individuals who are not.

Rights if work or goods and materials supplied are unsatisfactory
Refunds

If you have already paid a deposit to a builder and the work has not yet commenced and the trader is in breach of contract then you should be entitled to a refund of monies owed. If work has started then it is seen as reasonable that you allow the trader to rectify the fault, unless there is a specific reason why this should not be the case, i.e. the work has been left in such a dangerous condition that you feel that another builder is appropriate.

Replacement or repair

If you buy goods from a trader who installs them for you, you can ask the trader to replace or repair the goods free of charge if they are faulty or if they were installed without reasonable care or skill. You can ask for a refund if it is impossible to replace or repair the goods.

Compensation

You may be entitled to compensation if the work was not carried out in a reasonable time or with reasonable skill or negligence is apparent.

If you have incurred additional expenses as a result of faulty workmanship or goods then you may also be entitled to compensation. In the first instance you should contact the trader to solve the problem. Make sure all documents and other evidence have been retained.

If you cannot agree responsibility with the trader you should ascertain whether or not the trader is a member of a conciliation or mediation service. It may be necessary also to obtain an expert opinion. If the matter cannot be resolved then the last resort is the small claims court.

Organisations that deal with complaints against builders
Architects Registration Board

All architects must belong to the ARB and follow their code of conduct. They can be contacted on 020 7580 5861.

Royal Institute of British Architects (RIBA)

Almost all architects belong to RIBA which has an internal scheme to deal with arbitration and conciliation. They can be contacted on 0906 580 5533

Federation of Master Builders. The Master Bond Scheme

The FMB gives advice on how to choose a builder and details of its members in your area. It has a complaints procedure and an independent arbitration service. The MasterBond Scheme is part of the FMB. Builders who are members of the scheme are according to following its principles and practices. Their work is covered by a warranty scheme which is backed by an insurance company. There is an extra charge to be covered by this warranty.

In all cases, you should choose a reputable builder who is a member of such a federation. This will give you added protection. To find out about the FMB or the MasterBond scheme go to www.fmb.org.uk or 020 7242 7583.

Saving for Christmas

There are a number of ways of saving for Christmas. After the Farepak debacle in which many consumers lost money the need for so und advice is paramount. The following are considered safe methods of saving for Christmas, each with their own particular advantages and disadvantages outlined.

Standard bank and building society accounts

- You get interest on your money
- You sometimes get a bonus
- Your money is protected up to a limit
- Its up to you when you take your money out
- They will not collect money from your home
- They do not pay out in vouchers
- You do not have to buy from a particular shop or supplier

In short, saving with a bank or building society is perhaps the safest way of ensuring that you will keep hold of your money!

Special building society Christmas account

- You get interest on your money
- You will get a bonus
- You may lose that bonus and have to close your account if you take the money out early
- Your money is protected up to a limit if the building society goes bust
- They do not pay out in vouchers
- Most pay out before Christmas
- You do not have to buy from a particular shop or supplier

Credit Union savings account

- You may get a dividend
- Sometimes credit unions will pay you a bonus
- They will not collect money from your home
- If the credit union in England, Scotland and Wales goes bust, you money is protected up to a set limit
- They do not pay out in vouchers
- It is up to you when you pay your money out
- You do not have to buy from a particular shop or supplier

Special credit union Christmas savings account

- You may get a dividend
- Sometimes credit unions will pay you a bonus
- If you take money out early you may lose the dividend or bonus and have to close the account
- If a credit union in England, Scotland or Wales goes bust, your money is protected up to a certain point. For Northern Ireland check with the Companies Register
- Some credit unions pay out in vouchers
- They will pay out just before Christmas
- You do not have to buy from a particular shop or supplier.

Christmas clubs with local shops

- You will not get interest on your money
- They do not pay a bonus
- It could be difficult for you to take money out before the run-up to Christmas
- They will not collect the money from your home
- If the shop closes or goes bust you are not protected and, just like Farepak, you are unlikely to get all or any of your money back

- They do not pay out in vouchers
- You will have to buy from a particular shop or supplier

Hamper schemes

- You will not get interest on your money
- You will get a bonus
- They will make it difficult for you to take your money out before the run-up to Christmas
- They will collect money from your home
- If the company goes bust you are unlikely to get all your money back
- They pay out in vouchers
- They will pay out just before Christmas
- You will have to buy from a particular shop or supplier

Supermarket stamp schemes for Christmas

- You will not get interest on your money
- You will get a bonus
- They will make it difficult for you to take your money out before Christmas
- They will not collect money from your home
- If the company goes bust you are unlikely to get your money back

****

Chapter 16

Consumer Law in Scotland

As discussed in the introduction to this book, many of the consumer laws referred to in this book apply to Scotland as well as the rest of the United Kingdom. However, there are some differences, notably in the use of the court system to obtain remedies.

Little of the Supply of Goods and Services Act 1982 applies to Scotland. However, consumers have similar rights under Scottish common law.

Scottish law gives consumers five years, as opposed to six, after a purchase to take action if a problem has been discovered.

Consumers in Scotland and those who have bought items in Scotland have significantly different legal rights in the Scottish court system. For civil disputes, people take action mainly in the Sheriff Courts. Most consumer disputes are heard under a special small claims part of the 'summary cause' proceedings which, like the small claims procedure in the English, Welsh and Northern Irish county courts, is designed to be used without the need for solicitors. It has a maximum limit of £750. It is also possible to bring an action under a normal (and more formal) 'summary cause' proceedings up to a maximum of £1500. Above this limit, consumers have to use the 'ordinary cause' proceedings in the Sheriff Court, or, if they choose, the Outer House of the Court Session.

Court proceedings in the Scottish Courts do differ considerably from the rest of the United Kingdom. Trading Standards Departments in Scotland enforce criminal consumer laws in the same way as the rest of the

UK. They do not prosecute offenders themselves but investigate the facts and submit reports to the Procurator Fiscal where necessary. It is the Procurator Fiscal who decides whether or not prosecution is in the public interest. Claims for compensation for aggrieved consumers can be submitted by the Trading Standards Department in their report to the procurator Fiscal.

Scottish Criminal Law requires that most evidence is corroborated i.e. evidence is provided from two independent sources.

This is a very brief overview of the main differences between Scottish law and the rest of the UK. Separate publications deal with Scottish Consumer law in more depth.

****

Sample letters of complaint

Draft Letter: How to Complain About Poor Workmanship

Dear

{Insert Job and date}

I am writing to complain about the poor standard of workmanship I received in relation to the above job. As evidence of this I enclose a list of the problems. The work was clearly not carried out with reasonable care and skill (as required by section 13 Supply of Goods and Services Act) and, as such, amounts to a breach of contract.

Unless and until, these matters are rectified, I shall be withholding the balance of the contract price. Furthermore, if you do not put matters right within two weeks (or such other period as we may agree) I shall get another contractor to do it.

I will obtain a few quotations from reputable contractors and if the cost of the cheapest exceeds the balance of the contract price, I shall claim the extra from you by way of damages.

I will also report the matter to the Association, of which I note you are a member.

I await hearing from you.

Yours

Draft Letter: How to Complain By Withholding Payment

Dear

I am writing to notify you about why, and on what basis I am Withholding £ from the amount owing on my account.

On {date} I entered into a contract with   for the   of The   contract   price   was   £   And   I   paid   using   my card (see enclosed copy page from my card account).

{Explain nature of problem (eg defective service/goods))
{Explain why matter has not been resolved by the supplier (eg not acknowledging complaint or gone out of business))

As the cash price of the goods/service was Over £100 and as I paid using my   card, you, as the card issuer, are liable to the same extent as the supplier (section 75 Consumer Credit Act). Consequently, as   {name of supplier) has not satisfied my claim for breach of contract, I am legally entitled to withhold money representing the amount of my claim from you, and you cannot charge me interest on it.

To explain why I am withholding £   , I enclose photocopies of three quotations I have obtained as to the cost of putting matters rights. You will see that £   is the amount of the cheapest. Please acknowledge receipt of this letter, and confirm you will not be charging interest on £   withheld (unless and until the supplier actually satisfies my claim).

I await hearing from you.

Yours

Draft Letter: How to Complain About Holidays

Dear _____

{Location and Dates of Holiday}
Name in which booking was made
Hotel Name
Resort
Departure Date
Booking Reference Number

I am writing to complain about the above holiday from which I have just returned with my family. It was most disappointing. I enclose a list of our complaints. The main one was the fact that the (accommodation/facilities) was/were not _____ as described in the brochure (see enclosed photocopy extract from the brochure). Instead the (accommodation/facilities) was/were _____
I immediately contacted your representative at the resort, but he/she was unable to resolve the matter. He/she apologised and told me to complain when I got home. As our holiday was a package, the Package Travel Regulations 1992 apply to it. Under these regulations you are liable to compensate us for the problems we encountered and for the distress and disappointment we suffered as a result. If this matter cannot be resolved amicably, I shall send a copy of this letter and enclosures to ABTA (of which I note you are a member). (Also, if, as I suspect, the misdescription in the brochure was made 'knowingly' or 'recklessly' by you, you will have committed a criminal offence under the Trade Descriptions Act. Accordingly, I will report it to the trading standards department of my local authority for investigation).
I await hearing from you.

Draft Letter: How to Complain By Cancelling an Order

Dear _____

(Upate/Nature of Order)

I am writing to cancel the above order which I placed with you {include appropriate means of distance communication eg over the telephone)

As the contract was made at a distance, it is governed by the Distance Selling Regulations 2000. Under these regulations I have a cancellation period of seven working days from receipt of the goods.

The goods were delivered to my home yesterday, but when I unpacked them I realised that they were not appropriate for my needs. This is why I am canceling the contract. Consequently, please return the deposit I paid, and arrange to collect the goods at your earliest convenience.

Unless and until I receive written notice from you about collection and in any event, a refund of my deposit I will keep the contract goods. I will, of course, take reasonable care of them pending collection.

Under the Distance Selling Regulations, notice of cancellation which is posted is deemed effective on the date of posting. I will be posting this letter today, so please treat cancellation as effective from today's date.

I await hearing from you.

Yours

Draft letter-Distance Selling Regulations 2000. Not yet received goods/Cancel order

Owner/managers name

Address

Dear

Date

Re: Consumer Protection (Distance Selling) Regulations 2000

On (insert date) I ordered (goods). I received the goods on (date)/I have not yet received the goods.

Under the Consumer protection (Distance Selling) Regulations 2000 I am entitled to a seven day cooling off period, starting from the day I bought the goods. I am therefore writing to cancel the order and request that you provide a full refund within 30 days.

Please contact me within 14 days to arrange collection/return of goods.

Yours sincerely

Useful Addresses

Advertising Standards Authority

Mid City Place
71 High Holborn
London
WC1V 6QT

Tel: 020 7492 2222

Fax: 020 7242 3696

http://www.asa.org.uk

Association of British Travel Agents (ABTA)

ABTA Ltd
30 Park Street
London
SE1 9EQ

Tel: 0901 201 5050

http://www.abta.com

Association of Independent Tour Operators (AITO)

133A St Margaret's Road
Twickenham
Middlesex
TN1 1RG
020 8744 9280
http://www.aito.co.uk/

Association of Manufacturers of Domestic Electrical Appliances

Rapier House
40-46 Lamb's Conduit Street, London WC1N 3NW, United Kingdom
020 7405 0666
http://www.amdea.org.uk/index.asp

Association of British Insurers

Association of British Insurers
51 Gresham Street
London
EC2V 7HQ
www.abi.org.uk
020 7600 3333

British Standards Institution

389 Chiswick High Road
London
W4 4AL
United Kingdom
020 8996 2001

http://www.bsigroup.co.uk/en/

Chartered Institute of Arbitrators,
12 Bloomsbury Square, London WC1A 2LP
Tel 020 7421 7444.

Consumers Association (Which?)

Which?
2 Marylebone Road
London
NW1 4DF

http://www.which.co.uk/

Citizens Advice Consumer Service (Formerly Consumer Direct)
0845 404 0505
www.adviceguide.org.uk

The Consumer Credit Association (CCA)
CCA
Queens House
Queens Road
Chester
CH1 3BQ

Tel: 01244 312044
Fax: 01244 318035

email: complaints@ccauk.org
Website: www.ccauk.org

Consumer Credit Trade Association (CCTA)
Suite 4
The Wave
1 View Croft Road
Shipley
West Yorkshire
BD17 7DU

Tel: 01274 714959
Fax: 0845 257 1199
email: info@ccta.co.uk
Website: www.ccta.co.uk

Finance and Leasing Association (FLA)

Imperial House
15-19 Kingsway
London
WC2B 6UN

Tel: 020 7836 6511
fax 020 7420 9600
email: info@ fla.org.uk
Website: www.fla.org.uk

Office of Fair Trading

08457 224499

http://www.oft.gov.uk/

Radio, Electrical and Television Retailers Association

Retra House, St Johns Terrace, 1 Ampthill Street, Bedford, MK42 9EY
01234 269110
http://www.retra.co.uk/

Scottish Motor Traders Association

Palmerston House
10 The Loan

South Queensferry
EH30 9NS

0131 331 5510

http://www.smta.co.uk/

The Direct Marketing Association

70 Margaret Street

London W1W 8SS

020 7291 3300

http://www.dma.org.uk/content/home.asp

Index

ABTA, 79, 81, 82, 83, 129, 132
Actions before applying to court, 93
Advertising Standards Authority, 48, 102, 132
Aggressive Selling, 66
Alterations to the holiday, 82
Alternative Dispute Resolution, 6, 88
Arbitration, 6, 89
Architects Registration Board, 121
Association of Independent Tour Operators, 83, 132
Auctions, 45

Bank charges, 115
Banks and building societies, 114, 115
British Bankers Association, 115
Builders, 121
Buying at auction, 113
Buying goods, 41, 100
Buying goods in the European Union, 100
Buying on the doorstep, 4, 41

Cancellation of building work, 119
Cancelling a credit agreement, 43
Cancelling a timeshare agreement, 103
Cancelling an agreement, 4, 42
Chargeback, 21, 22, 23
Chartered Institute of Arbitrators, 91, 133
Christmas clubs, 123
Commencing a claim, 91, 93
Communication and Internet Services Adjudication Scheme (CISAS, 112

Communication and Internet Services Adjudication Scheme (CISAS), 112
Conciliation, 6, 89
Conditional sale transaction, 24
Consumer credit, 49
Consumer Credit Act 1974, 21, 49, 83
Consumer Credit Act 1974., 49, 83
Consumer Credit Association, 5, 60, 134
Consumer Credit Trade Association, 5, 61, 134
Consumer Direct, 9, 42, 78, 91, 101, 103, 109, 110, 113, 134
Consumer Protection (Distance Selling) Regulations 2000, 39, 44
Consumer Protection Act 1987, 3, 12, 27, 67, 76
Consumer Protection from Unfair Trading Regulations 2008, 40, 66
Consumer Transactions (Restrictions on Statements) Order 1976, 37
Consumers in Scotland, 125
Contracts for buying goods, 12
Contracts for services, 12
Contracts for the sale of land, 45
Control of Misleading Advertising Regulations 1988., 67
Credit Union, 123

Damage to private property, 28
Dealing with Builders, 7, 119
Defective goods, 5, 16
Defective Goods, 3, 16
Deny liability for a product, 34
Denying Liability, 4
Department of Enterprise, 75
Direct Marketing Association, 48, 136
Direct Selling Association, 44
Distance selling, 12
Distance Selling, 4, 14, 39, 41, 44, 46, 47, 49, 130, 131

Distance Selling Regulations 2000, 14, 41, 46, 49, 130, 131
Driving overseas, 118
Dry cleaning, 110
Dry Cleaning Technology Centre, 111

European Consumer Centres, 102
European Consumer Complaint Form, 102
European Directives, 37
Extended warranties, 32
Extended warranties for electrical goods, 32
Extortionate credit bargains, 64

Faulty goods, 43, 101
Faulty goods or services, 43
Federation of Master Builders, 121
Finance and Leasing Association, 5, 61, 135
Financial Ombudsman Service, 23, 115, 119
Financial services, 45
Financial Services Authority, 108, 119
Financial Services Compensation Scheme (FCS), 116
Fitness of purpose, 18
Food poisoning, 85
Food safety, 8, 85
Food Safety Act Amendment Regulations 2004, 85

General Food Regulations 2004, 85
General Product Safety Regulations 2005, 77
General Unfair Practices, 66
Guarantees, 3, 17, 31, 101
Hamper schemes, 124
Hire purchase, 24

Hired goods, 65

Insolvency of the tour operator, 83

Legal protection with guarantees and warranties, 31

Mail Order Traders Association, 48
MasterBond scheme, 121
Mediation, 6, 90, 91
Merchantable quality, 17
Misleading Prices, 66
Mobile phones, 111
Motor cycle insurance, 118
Motor Insurance, 116
Motor Insurers Bureau (MIB), 118
Motor Insurers Information Centre, 117

Office of Fair Trading (OFT, 75
Office of the Telecommunications Ombudsman (OTELO), 112
Ombudsman schemes, 90
Overbooking of flights, 82

Package holidays, 12, 45, 79, 81
Package Holidays, 6, 79, 83
Package Travel, 6, 79, 83, 129
Package Travel, Package Holidays and Package Tours Regulations 1992,
    79
Periodical Publishers Association (PPA) schemes, 47
Personal injury, 28
Pyramid schemes, 69

Royal Institute of British Architects (RIBA), 121

Safe Home Ordering Protection Scheme, 47
Sale and Supply of Goods Act 1994, 13
Sale of Goods Act 1979, 13, 16, 17, 33, 35, 113
Saving for Christmas, 7, 122
Scotland, 7, 75, 123, 125
Sending the goods back, 20
Small Claims, 7, 91
Statements made in holiday brochures, 81
Stolen vehicle, 117
Supply of Goods (implied terms) Act 1973, 24
Supply of Goods and Services Act 1982, 13, 125

Textile Services Association, 110
The 1990 Food Safety Act, 85
The Banking Code, 114
The contract of sale, 13
The law of contract, 12
The Law Society, 91
The Master Bond Scheme, 121
The Office of Fair Trading, 84
The right to clear information, 45
The Small Claims Court, 7, 91
The Timeshare Consumers Association, 104
The Unfair Contract Terms Act 1977, 35
Timeshare, 7, 45, 102, 104
Toy Safety Regulations 1995, 77
Trade Descriptions, 9, 66, 67, 79, 129
Travel Insurance, 7, 106

Unreasonable demands, 70
Unsafe Goods, 5
Unsolicited goods, 39
Unsolicited Goods and Services act 1971, 39
Use of materials when carrying out repairs, 25

Warranties, 3, 17, 31